FLYNT•COOTER

READING INVENTORY

FOR THE CLASSROOM

SECOND EDITION

E. Sutton Flynt
Pittsburg State University

Robert B. Cooter, Jr.
Texas Christian University

Illustrations by Deborah S. Flynt

28.50

GSP

Gorsuch Scarisbrick, Publishers
Scottsdale, Arizona

Publisher: John W. Gorsuch
Editor: Nils Anderson
Developmental Editor: Gay L. Pauley
Production Editor: Mary B. Cullen
Interior Illustration: Deborah S. Flynt
Cover Design: Kevin Kall
Typesetting: Ash Street Typecrafters, Inc.

Gorsuch Scarisbrick, Publishers
8233 Via Paseo del Norte, F400
Scottsdale, Arizona 85258

10 9 8 7 6 5 4 3 2 1

ISBN 0-89787-538-9

Printed in the United States of America.

▃ CONTENTS ▃

EXAMINER'S ASSESSMENT PROTOCOLS   53

FORM B

SENTENCES FOR INITIAL PASSAGE SELECTION   89
NARRATIVE PASSAGES   93

EXAMINER'S ASSESSMENT PROTOCOLS   113

FORM C

SENTENCES FOR INITIAL PASSAGE SELECTION   149
EXPOSITORY PASSAGES   153

EXAMINER'S ASSESSMENT PROTOCOLS   167

▟▚ FORM D ▞▙

EXPOSITORY PASSAGES, Levels 10–12   197

EXAMINER'S ASSESSMENT PROTOCOLS   205

APPENDIX: OPTIONAL MISCUE GRIDS   219

ACKNOWLEDGMENTS

Reading Inventory for the Classroom (*RIC*) was developed to provide in-service and preservice teachers with a simple, straightforward means of assessing student reading development. The following individuals and groups provided a great deal of assistance during the development and fine-tuning of the inventory. As a result of their insight and suggestions, the *RIC* is a better, more effective inventory.

We would like to extend our appreciation to the following individuals: Claudia Cornett, Wittenberg University; Shirley Freed, Andrews University; Carolyn M. Griffin, Mabee Reading Clinic; Victoria J. Risko, Vanderbilt University; M.K. Gillis, Southwest Texas State University; D. Ray Reutzel, Brigham Young University; Linda Gambrell, University of Maryland; MaryLou Curley, San Antonio Independent School District; Patrice Werner, Southwest Texas State University; Bill King, Westside Elementary School; the Chapter I Teachers, San Antonio Independent School District; the faculty and students at Westside Elementary School; the faculty and students at George Nettels Elementary School; and Nils Anderson, Mary Cullen, and Gay Pauley of Gorsuch Scarisbrick, Publishers. Special thanks to John Lidh and Laser Precision for the use of information about OTDRs.

Finally, we dedicate this book to our families, who never got tired of listening to the passages or our ideas.

E. Sutton Flynt
Robert B. Cooter

INTRODUCTION

In recent years a rather spirited dialogue has been taking place among reading educators regarding the role and nature of reading assessment. Valencia and Pearson (1987) captured an important point of consensus in the debate with the following statement:

> What we need are not just new and better tests. We need a new framework for thinking about assessment, one in which educators begin by considering types of decisions needed and the level of impact of those decisions. (729)

We attempted to use the spirit of this statement as a guide in the design of the Flynt–Cooter *Reading Inventory for the Classroom*. Some important questions teachers ask (and their answers) helped guide the construction of this instrument.

We addressed the first question: *What decisions are required of classroom teachers, specialists, and clinicians in the initial assessment of students' reading development?* To answer this question candidly and consistently, one might first identify her or his theoretical and instructional orientation. Our view of learning is drawn from transactional theory (Rosenblatt, 1978; Goodman, 1985; Smith, 1982), which is described by Reutzel and Cooter (1992) as emphasizing "that the reader, the text, and the social-situational context are inextricably linked and are transformed as a result of the reading event" (40). Similarly we adopt a view of teaching compatible with that espoused by such process-oriented and holistic educators as Holdaway (1979), Harste et al. (1984), and Newman (1985). Thus we feel that reading assessment should offer the teacher insights into student interests, attitudes, and motivation (affective considerations), background knowledge, types of text that students may have difficulty reading, and learning or teaching situations that may be problematic. This perspective contrasts sharply with more traditional views of reading assessment that tend to focus on the testing of discrete subskills with little or no attention to affective or social-situational contexts. In this instrument we only attempt to address a selected aspect of the affective domain, background knowledge, as well as the reader's ability to decode and comprehend narrative and expository texts.

We wish to note that at present many teachers may still be in a transitional mode of teaching (Reutzel and Cooter, 1992), moving gradually toward holistic teaching while still using many traditional materials and practices. This inventory, therefore, retains some traditional methods and descriptions easily identifiable to teachers in an early stage of transition as well as naturalistic assessment methods and descriptions that are more consistent with current thinking about assessment.

The kinds of teaching and intervention decisions possible with the *Reading Inventory for the Classroom* (*RIC*) relate to such areas as:

- use of decoding strategies

- reading aspects of print (selected words, punctuation, fluency)

- attention to story elements and content elements

- literal and inferential comprehension

- miscue recording and pattern determination

From these and other data derived from the inventory, teachers working with at-risk students can begin to make decisions related to the kinds of reading materials that can be used, the pacing of instruction, the emphasis of instruction, and the need for student collaborative opportunities. Data gathered using the *RIC* should of course be viewed only as one part of a comprehensive assessment. Results can be used as part of a student's portfolio, as a starting point for instruction, or as evidence to be shared in staffings that focus on whether students should be placed in special programs.

We also addressed the question for teachers that naturally follows: *What is the level of impact of these decisions?* This question has many interpretations based on the teacher's professional assignment. For the classroom reading teacher, the level of impact usually relates to the matching of reading materials and learning opportunities to the student's interests and performance abilities. For reading specialists and special program teachers, the level of impact involves the preceding decisions plus decision making related to the selection and retention of students in intervention programs.

In summary there are several important purposes of process-oriented reading assessment that can be addressed in part through use of this inventory. Werner (1991), in her discussion of purposes of naturalistic assessment as applied to the writing process, lists several key points that summarize our subsidiary needs: (1) to show what stages students are in developmentally and to create an initial record of progress, (2) to determine areas of strength and need for planning instruction, and (3) to help teachers learn more about the reading process through interaction with students.

WHAT IS THE FLYNT–COOTER *READING INVENTORY FOR THE CLASSROOM?*

The Flynt–Cooter *RIC* is an informal reading inventory intended for reading levels from preprimer through grade 12. It was developed to meet the needs of professionals interested in assessing the reading competencies of students in the public or private schools, intervention programs, or clinical settings. The primary purpose of the inventory is to assist teachers in the placement of students with appropriate reading and instructional materials. Additionally the inventory can be used for educating preservice and in-service teachers in reading assessment and interpretation of results.

DESCRIPTION OF THE *RIC*

The inventory itself begins with an interest/attitude questionnaire designed to assist the examiner in establishing a rapport with the student and to gather information about socially relevant factors that may be influencing the student's interest in reading. It also has the potential to suggest topics and/or materials for use in the classroom and/or remedial setting that may interest the student. Both a primary-level interview (p. 25) and an upper-level interview (p. 27) are provided.

The assessment portion of the inventory is divided into four forms: A, B, C, and D. Each of Forms A, B, and C, in turn, is composed of three sections: sentences to determine initial passage selection, the reading passages themselves, and the accompanying assessment protocols. Form D has no accompanying sentences for initial passage selection and will be discussed separately.

In Forms A, B, and C, the section entitled "Sentences for Initial Passage Selection" is a series of sentences designed to help examiners choose the initial passage, from Level 1 through Level 9, with which students will begin reading. (Instructions are provided later for administering the preprimer assessment to students who do not perform well on Level 1 sentences.) We have used sentences rather than the familiar word lists because reading sentences is closer to the actual act of reading than reading words in isolation. The sentences not only provide insights into how the reader approaches unfamiliar words but also provide a brief view of the reader's competence at varying levels of difficulty. If, as recommended, the examiner records the oral miscues (reading errors) students make while reading the sentences, then this information proves helpful in formulating ideas about the student's decoding and comprehension instructional needs. The words used in Form A sentences are drawn in part from the Form A narrative passages, as is true for Forms B and C. Thus, if an examiner is going to use Form A, then only sentences in Form A should be used to determine the starting point for reading the passages.

The reading selections were written or adapted by the authors and reflect what we perceive to be some of the interests of the students at the various age levels represented. Topics for the passages were selected based on our conversations with the school-age students we have worked with in recent years, as well as with our own children. This new edition of the *RIC* includes Levels PP and P in Forms A and B and also a new Form D, which includes grade levels 10, 11, and 12. Special instructions for administering these new passages are provided in the next section. All passages are leveled such that Level PP corresponds to beginning first grade reading difficulty and Level 12 corresponds to twelfth grade difficulty. Forms A and B are narrative (story) passages, while Forms C and D are expository (factual/content-oriented) passages. Passage difficulty was determined using a combination of means including the Fry Readability Graph (1968), the Harris-Jacobsen Readability Formula (1975), and our own judgment. Notwithstanding the widely known limitations of readability formulas, the passages are within the assigned ranges. As with all assessment instruments and procedures, the examiner needs to use observation and judgment to interpret any findings concerning a student's reading level and abilities.

Following the reading selections in each of the forms are examiner's protocol forms for analysis of student reading ability. The protocols include an introductory prereading statement, comprehension questions, a miscue analysis grid, and a final section for analyzing results and determining whether or not to continue testing. For narrative passages, each of the comprehension questions is labeled according to story grammar element (holistic/ naturalistic) and hierarchical level (traditional view) of comprehension. For expository passages, each question is labeled by a designation we refer to as "expository grammar element" (based on the work of Meyer & Freedle, 1984) and traditional levels of comprehension.

A unique feature of the *RIC* is the inclusion of a miscue grid for each passage. Based on the seminal work of Goodman and Burke (1969, 1987), these grids, once completed by the examiner, will assist examiners in identifying error patterns made by students that will, in turn, lead to intervention decisions. Grids focus primarily on aspects of word identification and the use of context. Finally, a scoring chart is provided at the end of each protocol to assist in determining whether or not to continue the assessment.

The procedure for using these protocols is discussed more fully in the next section. A scored student example is provided on pages 13–18.

WHO SHOULD USE THE FLYNT–COOTER *RIC?*

The *RIC* is appropriate for both preservice (students enrolled in teacher education programs) and in-service teachers, and any other practicing professionals involved with students with reading needs. We feel it provides valuable insights into reading development, especially in the reading of connected text, word analysis, story and content comprehension, and miscue analysis. Classroom teachers using basal reading programs will find the inventory quite useful in basal placement. Teachers implementing literature-based reading programs will find the inventory helpful in planning collaborative learning activities involving reading, planning minilessons, and determining which non-negotiable skills (Reutzel and Cooter, 1992) need further development (these are subskills necessary to teach because of state or local mandates, testing programs, and/or teacher judgment about reading development). The *RIC* can also provide a valuable starting place for portfolio assessment profiles. In an intervention or clinical education setting, it can be used as part of an assessment training program as well as an investigative tool for research purposes.

HOW THE FLYNT–COOTER *RIC* DIFFERS FROM OTHER INFORMAL READING INVENTORIES

From the outset, we wanted to create an inventory that is easy to use, focuses on identifying student strengths, helps teachers plan for instruction, and reflects the current state of knowledge concerning the assessment of reading processes. We also wanted to develop an instrument that is traditional in appearance and may be used by reading educators with a more traditional view of reading education. The second edition of the *RIC* has a number of features that help satisfy these goals.

- *Emergent reader rubric*—The *RIC* contains a unique method for assessing prereading capabilities using holistic instructional procedures.

- *Miscue analysis grids*—Informed instruction is based on patterns of behavior, not one-time errors in oral reading. Each passage protocol includes a miscue analysis grid containing a facsimile of the passage, space for marking oral reading miscues, and columns for tallying numbers of miscue types. These grids facilitate efficient identification of error patterns and assist the teacher in planning intervention sessions based on student need.

- *Interest/attitude inventory*—This inventory is designed to gather affective information about students.

- *High-interest passages*—The passages in this inventory reflect some of the prominent interests of students in elementary and secondary school settings.

- *Longer passages*—Passages are longer than typical instruments to allow for full development of story information and context. This creates more authentic ("real reading") situations to be observed.

- *Passage retellings*—Many authorities in reading complain that comprehension assessment has become an "interrogation." The use of passage retellings seems to be a more naturalistic approach to assessment, much less stressful for students and usually more informative for the examiner. Retellings are used at all levels of the inventory; then only those questions are asked that relate to text information not recounted by the student.

- *Story grammar analyses*—Recently introduced holistic views of reading comprehension have endorsed the story grammar perspective (for example, setting, characterization, story problem, resolution, theme). Each question in the silent reading/retelling section of Forms A and B (narrative selections) is keyed to story grammar categories, as well as to traditional hierarchical labels (literal, inferential, and so on).

- *Expository text grammars*—Just as narrative passages are keyed to the story grammar perspective, expository selections in Forms C and D are keyed to text-types (expository text grammars) based on the work of Meyer and Freedle (1984), as well as to traditional comprehension labels.

ADMINISTRATION AND SCORING PROCEDURES

STEP 1: INTEREST/ATTITUDE INTERVIEW

One of the most important, and often ignored, aspects of reading assessment is the affective domain. Affect involves interest, attitude, and motivational factors related to reading success. We include an Interest/Attitude Interview to assist examiners in learning more about students' background knowledge, interests, and motivations that may relate to reading success. Information from this brief survey should be used in the selection of reading materials that will be appealing to the student.

Two versions of the Interest/Attitude Interview are included: Primary Form and Upper Level Form. The Primary Form is intended for students in grades 1 and 2, and the Upper Level Form is intended for grades 3 through 12. In each case the examiner begins with the introductory statement provided on the form, then proceeds by asking each of the questions. It is the intention of the authors that examiners use these questions as a springboard for discussion, not simply as a rote exercise. Similarly, examiners should feel free to disregard any questions they feel are inappropriate.

Research on the affective domain and how it relates to reading success is rather sparse, and recommendations for using data derived from an interview of this sort are few. However, most teachers/examiners find that information derived from the Interest/Attitude Interview can be beneficial in several ways. First, information about reading interests can help the teacher select reading materials that are appealing to the student, and choose texts most likely matched to students' background knowledge and vocabulary. Second, information derived from questions related to reading and study habits at home can provide teachers with insights and appropriate suggestions for parents. Third, students often help teachers understand what their strengths and needs are in reading through the students' answers to such questions as "What makes a person a good reader?" and "What causes a person to not be a good reader?" The Interest/Attitude Interview will not tell teachers everything they need to know about students' abilities, but it *will* help in finding an informed departure point for quality reading experiences.

STEP 2: INITIAL PASSAGE SELECTION SENTENCES

Begin by having students read the set of placement sentences at the beginning of the selected form of the inventory (A, B, or C). We suggest having students begin reading sentences two grade levels below their current grade placement, if possible. This will help avoid potential student frustration caused by starting with passages that are too difficult. If the student is in either grade 1, 2, or 3, begin with Level 1 sentences. (*Note:* If students do not perform well on the Level 1 sentences, see the instructions on pages 8–11 for administering the Preprimer and Primer passages.) **Have students continue reading sets of placement sentences until they miss two words or more, then stop. The highest level of placement sentences read with zero errors should be the level of the first passage to be read by the student.** For students who have no errors through Level 9, begin with Form D, Level 10.

STEP 3: READING PASSAGES

As mentioned previously, students should begin reading the passage indicated by their performance on the initial passage selection sentences. Examiners should place in front of the student a copy of the passage from which the student will read. In schools where a great deal of assessment takes place, we recommend that the student copies be laminated.

Examiners should turn to the corresponding protocol form for that passage and follow along. **Permission is granted to teachers purchasing the Flynt–Cooter *RIC* to duplicate these protocol forms for their own classroom needs.** Note that each protocol is divided into Parts I, II, and III. A step-by-step description is offered for each section.

Part I: Silent Reading Comprehension

1. Read the background statement aloud and say that you will ask for a retelling of the passage after the student has read it silently. Then allow the student to read the passage once silently.

2. After the silent reading is complete, remove the passage and ask the student to retell the main points of the passage. Check off each question in Part I that is answered during the student's retelling. When the retelling is finished, ask any remaining questions that were not covered in the retelling or that need clarification. Any questions the student cannot answer are scored as silent reading comprehension errors and noted in the Part III summary section.

3. Because of the level of sophistication of students reading above the ninth grade, we recommend that students who are asked to read passages 10D, 11D, or 12D only read the passage silently. We feel it is unnecessary at these levels to assess students' oral reading behaviors. However, for those who wish to conduct oral reading at these levels, a grid has been provided.

Part II: Oral Reading and Analysis of Miscues

Next, have the student read the passage orally up to the *oral reading stop-marker* (*//*) noted on the protocol grid. Note any miscues on the passage facsimile portion of the grid. A description of miscues and how to mark them on the protocol is included in the next section. It is based on the work of Clay (1985) and Reutzel and Cooter (1992). Note that the grid should not be completed during the oral reading (completion is probably not possible in any case), but should be completed *after* the assessment session has been concluded with the student. Miscues should be marked on the passage facsimile during the oral reading, errors totaled, and a decision made (in Part III) as to whether or not to continue the assessment.

Miscues and Coding for Passages

- *Mispronunciation*

  Student incorrectly pronounces a word. Mispronunciations typically are non-words. Write the incorrect pronunciation above the word on the protocol.

  Student: *"The deg ran away."*

  Notation: The d**eg**og ran away.

- *Substitution*

  Student substitutes a real word or words for a word in the text. Draw a line through the word and write what the student said above it.

  Student: *"The tree was very high."*

  Notation: The ~~cloud~~ **tree** was very high.

- *Omission*

  If no word (or words) is given, the error is noted by circling the word(s) omitted on the protocol.

  Notation: The cloud was (very) high.

- *Self-correction*

  Student corrects a miscue himself. Self-corrections are noted by writing "SC," but should not be counted as errors in the final tally, unless the student never correctly pronounces the word.

  Student: *"The money . . . the monkey was funny."*

  Notation: The m(SC)onkey was funny.

- *Insertion*

  A word is added that is *not* in the text. An insertion symbol (^) is recorded between the two appropriate words, and the inserted word is written above the insertion symbol.

  Student: *He'll want to have a look in the mirror.*

  Notation: He'll want to ^have a^ look in the mirror.

- *Teacher assistance*

  The student is "stuck" on a word and the teacher pronounces it. Record the incident as "TA" (teacher-assisted). This error is also counted when the student asks for help during silent reading.

  Notation: automobile (TA)

- *Repetition*

  The student repeats a word or series of words. A repetition is recorded by underlining the word(s) repeated. This category is recorded as additional observational data but *does not* figure in the determination of whether to continue testing or not. Therefore, in determining the number of miscues a student makes on a passage, repetitions are not a part of the final tally.

  Student: *The boy wanted to wanted to go to the show.*

  Notation: The boy <u>wanted to</u> go to the show.

- *Meaning disruption: A special consideration*

  Working with students, we have observed that some miscues are much more disruptive to comprehension than others. For instance, insertions often do not significantly alter reading comprehension, but mispronunciations typically do. Thus we have included a Meaning Disruptions column on the Miscue Grid to encourage examiners to reflect on the severity of each miscue as it pertains to reading comprehension. Note that this is *not a miscue type;* rather, it is a point for the examiner to determine whether each miscue adversely affects the student's comprehension. If it does, a mark should be placed in this column to alert you that the student may be word calling rather than attending to the message of the passage. As you summarize a student's performance and begin to make instructional decisions about the student's needs, this column should provide you with additional information related to reading comprehension.

Oral reading miscues should be noted on the passage facsimile as the student is reading. We recommend that the student's voice also be tape recorded during the retelling and oral reading to allow for convenient review at a later time, and to establish permanent audio records of the child's reading development. As noted, miscue grids should be completed after the assessment session with the child has been concluded.

Part III: Developmental/Performance Summary

The final section helps examiners determine whether or not to continue testing and identify the reading placement level. For silent reading comprehension and oral reading accuracy a three-tier system is used. In each case the examiner decides whether the passage appeared to be *easy, adequate,* or *too hard* for the student. These descriptors are based on the work of Powell (1969) and Betts (1946). *Easy* means that the passage can be read with few errors and the student requires no additional assistance from others in reading similar texts. The easy level is comparable to the independent reading level designation used in traditional informal reading inventories. *Adequate* means that students can read the passage effectively, but will likely require some help from another person to successfully comprehend the passage. The adequate level is comparable to the instructional designation used in traditional informal reading inventories. *Too hard* means that the passage difficulty is sufficient to cause the reader much anxiety and frustration. This level is sometimes called the frustration level in traditional inventories. We have used the designations easy, adequate, and too hard because we feel they describe the student's performance in simple terms that can be easily discussed with parents. **A student who scores at the too hard level in Silent Reading Comprehension should not proceed to any higher level passage.** Placement in reading material should be at the level just below the passage receiving a too hard judgment. Thus if a student first reaches a too hard score on Level 5 Silent Reading Comprehension, reading placement level for instructional purposes should be Level 4.

STEP 4: COMPLETING THE STUDENT SUMMARY

Immediately following the scored student sample is a copy of the *RIC* Student Summary. Like all other sections of this inventory, it may be duplicated by examiners for classroom assessment use. Examiners should complete this summary after the assessment session(s) has been completed in order to gather together information and begin to develop initial classroom intervention plans, should they be necessary.

The *RIC* is only a starting point in the assessment and intervention process. We encourage teachers and examiners embarking on intervention programs to begin with what students know, in order to continue sampling and gathering data about the student's reading abilities. This is what Marie Clay (1985) refers to as "roaming around the known." Clay suggests a two-week period of roaming around the known in her Reading Recovery Programme, the equivalent of about five hours spread over two weeks. This kind of continuing assessment, when used in conjunction with the *RIC,* yields rich descriptive information about the student. As stated in the final section of the Student Summary, we feel that this process should help the teacher and examiner learn more about the student's reading abilities, confirm or reject initial findings drawn from this inventory, and discover ways of helping students continue to grow as successful readers.

INSTRUCTIONS FOR ADMINISTERING
THE PREPRIMER (PP) AND PRIMER (P) PASSAGES

We have added passages for emergent readers to Forms A and B of the *RIC*. These passages have been given the conventional labels of Preprimer (PP) and Primer (P), but reflect a much more holistic view of early reading processes. We have drawn on recent research in emergent literacy (Clay, 1985; Sulzby, 1985, 1987; Morrow, 1993; Adams, 1994) to develop passages and procedures that can be used in beginning assessment in elementary classrooms. While information gained from administering these passages can be useful to teachers early in the school year and for periodic assessments, we feel that regular student–teacher interactions using authentic storybooks are necessary for more complete assessment profiles.

In developing these passages we have considered carefully the research of Cochrane and others (1984) and Sulzby (1985), who have attempted to chronicle the observable emergent reading developmental "milestones." To assist in the assessment of emergent readers, we have created checklists for the PP and P levels based on research findings in emergent literacy. The stages we have developed are listed below.

Stage 1: Early Connections to Reading—Describing Pictures

- Attends to and describes (labels) pictures in books
- Has a limited sense of story
- Follows verbal directions for this activity
- Uses oral vocabulary appropriate for age/grade level
- Displays attention span appropriate for age/grade level
- Responds to questions in an appropriate manner
- Appears to connect pictures (sees them as being interrelated)

Stage 2: Connecting Pictures to Form a Story

- Attends to pictures and develops oral stories across the pages of the book
- Uses only childlike or descriptive (storyteller) language to tell the story, rather than book language (i.e., Once upon a time...; There once was a little boy...)

Stage 3: Transitional Picture Reading

- Attends to pictures as a connected story
- Mixes storyteller language with book language

Stage 4: Advanced Picture Reading

- Attends to pictures and develops oral stories across the pages of the book
- Speaks as though reading the story (uses book language)

Stage 5: Early Print Reading

- Tells a story using the pictures
- Knows print moves from left to right, top to bottom
- Creates part of the text using book language and knows some words on sight

Stage 6: Early Strategic Reading

- Uses context to guess at some unknown words (guesses make sense)

- Notices beginning sounds in words and uses them in guessing unknown words

- Seems to sometimes use syntax to help identify words in print

- Recognizes some word parts, such as root words and affixes

Stage 7: Moderate Strategic Reading

- Sometimes uses context and word parts to decode words

- Self-corrects when making an oral reading miscue

- Retells the passage easily and may embellish the storyline

- Shows some awareness of vowel sounds

In attempting to provide passages at emergent reading levels that correspond in some meaningful way with current knowledge of emergent literacy, we chose a simple but informative format. At the Preprimer (PP) level, we have provided a wordless picture book format. In each case the story is told using a series of four illustrations that tell a story when read or retold sequentially. This format will enable examiners to learn whether the student has progressed through the first three or four stages of emergent reading as just outlined. Passages at the Primer (P) level also use the four-illustration format but include predictable text that tells the story. These passages enable the examiner to gain additional insights into the more advanced emergent reading stages outlined above.

We recommend that examiners begin with these passages if the student's performance on the placement sentences (see the following instructions) suggests that the Level 1 passages may be too difficult. Explain to students at both the PP and P levels that the four pictures tell a story. Ask the student to look at all four pictures first then retell the story by "reading" the pictures. We recommend that you transcribe the student's reading for later analysis. A tape recording of the session is quite helpful since you will probably have difficulty transcribing all that is said. If a student seems unable to tell a story from the pictures, ask the student to describe each picture. This will provide some insights into vocabulary knowledge, oral language skills, and whether a sense of story is developing. Further directions for administering Level PP and P passages and completing accompanying checklists are included with the assessment protocol forms (A & B) for each passage.

If the Student Cannot Read the Primer Level (P) Passage Adequately on the First Attempt . . . Then What?

Sometimes students making the developmental transition from advanced picture reading to early print reading are able to memorize text easily and repeat it verbatim, or nearly so. This sets up the opportunity for teaching them about one-to-one correspondence between spoken and written words and sounds. Therefore, if a student is unable to adequately read a passage aloud the first time, the examiner should read it aloud and then ask the student to try reading it again. If the student is able to do so, the examiner may assume that the student is transitioning into the early print reading stage. This would be a logical stopping point for the assessment.

INSTRUCTIONS FOR ADMINISTERING THE FORM D PASSAGES

In response to suggestions from educators, we have added a Form D to this edition of the *RIC*. These passages are designed for students who read above the ninth-grade level. Each level (10, 11, 12) corresponds to that level of sophistication associated with high school reading. All three passages are expository in nature and are administered similarly to Form C passages. The one difference we recommend is that students not be required to read a portion of the passage orally. We believe that the oral reading skills of students in the 10th grade and above do not offer insightful assessment data. Rather, we believe that silent reading comprehension is the most important variable to be assessed at these levels. For those individuals who want to assess oral reading at these levels, however, we have provided a Miscue Grid for each passage. Assessment of oral reading using this grid follows the guidelines discussed earlier.

SELECTED REFERENCES

Adams, M. J. (1994). *Beginning to read.* Cambridge, MA: MIT Press.

Betts, E. A. (1946). *Foundation of reading instruction.* New York: Academic Book Company.

Burke, C. (1987). Burke reading interview. In Y. Goodman, D. Watson, & C. Burke (Eds.), *Reading miscue inventory: Alternative procedures.* New York: Richard C. Owen.

Clay, M. M. (1985). *The early detection of reading difficulties* (3rd ed.). Auckland, New Zealand: Heinemann Educational Books, Inc.

Cochrane, O., Cochrane, D., Scalena, D., & Buchanan, E. (1984). *Reading, writing, and caring.* New York: Richard C. Owen.

Farr, R., & Tone, B. (1994). *Portfolio and performance assessment.* Fort Worth: Harcourt Brace.

Fry, E. (1968). Readability formula that saves time. *Journal of Reading, 11,* 513–516, 575–578.

Goodman, K. S. (1969). Analysis of oral reading miscues: Applied psycholinguistics. *Reading Research Quarterly, 5,* 9–30.

Goodman, K. S. (1985). Unity in reading. In H. Singer & R. B. Ruddell (Eds.), *Theoretical models and processes of reading,* 813–840. Newark, DE: International Reading Association, Inc.

Harris, A. J., & Jacobson, M. D. (1975). The Harris–Jacobson readability formulas. In A. J. Harris & E. R. Sipay (Eds.), *How to increase reading ability* (pp. 712–729). New York: Longman, Inc.

Harste, J. C., Woodward, V. A., & Burke, C. L. (1984). *Language stories and literacy lessons.* Portsmouth, NH: Heinemann Educational Books, Inc.

Hill, B. C., & Ruptic, C. (1994). *Practical aspects of authentic assessment: Putting the pieces together.* Norwood, MA: Christopher-Gordon.

Holdaway, D. (1979). *Foundations of literacy.* Sydney: Ashton Scholastic.

Meyer, B. J. F., & Freedle, R. O. (1984). Effects of discourse type on recall. *American Educational Research Journal, 21*(1), 121–143.

Morrow, L. M. (1993). *Literacy development in the early years* (2nd ed.). Boston: Allyn and Bacon.

Newman, J. M. (Ed.). (1985). *Whole language: Theory in use.* Portsmouth, NH: Heinemann Educational Books, Inc.

Piaget, J. (1955). *The language and thought of the child.* New York: World.

Powell, W. R. (1969). Reappraising the criteria for interpreting informal inventories. In D. DeBoer (Ed.), *Reading diagnosis and evaluation* (pp. 100–109). Newark, DE: International Reading Association.

Puckett, M. B., & Black, J. K. (1994). *Authentic assessment of the young child.* New York: Merrill.

Reutzel, D. R., & Cooter, R. B. (1992). *Teaching children to read: From basals to books*. New York: Merrill, an imprint of Prentice Hall.

Rhodes, L. K., & Dudley-Marling, C. (1988). *Readers and writers with a difference*. Portsmouth, NH: Heinemann Educational Books, Inc.

Rosenblatt, L. M. (1978). *The reader, the text, and the poem*. Carbondale, IL: Southern Illinois University Press.

Smith, F. (1982). *Writing and the writer*. New York: Holt, Rinehart & Winston.

Sulzby, E. (1985). Children's emergent reading of favorite storybooks. *Reading Research Quarterly, 20,* 458–481.

Sulzby, E. (1987). *Simplified version of Sulzby's (1985) classification scheme for "Children's emergent reading of favorite storybooks."* Paper presented at the International Reading Association Conference, Anaheim, CA.

Sulzby, E. (1991). Assessment of emergent literacy: Storybook reading. *The Reading Teacher, 44*(7), 498–500.

Valencia, S., & Pearson, P. D. (1987). Reading assessment: Time for a change. *The Reading Teacher, 40*(8), 726–733.

Werner, P. H. (1991). *Purposes of reading/writing assessment: A process view.* Unpublished manuscript, Southwest Texas State University, San Marcos, TX.

SCORED
STUDENT EXAMPLE

(pages 14–18)

The following pages provide an example of a completed student assessment. This particular example is based on the Level 5 passage found in Form A.

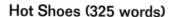

Hot Shoes (325 words)

PART I: SILENT READING COMPREHENSION

Background Statement: "This story is about how one group of boys feel about their athletic shoes. Read this story to find out how important special shoes are to playing sports. Read it carefully because I will ask you to tell me about it when you finish."

Teacher Directions: Once the student completes the silent reading, say, "Tell me about the story you just read." Check off any answers to the following questions that the student provides during the retelling. Ask all remaining questions not addressed during the retelling.

Questions/Answers

Story Grammar Element/ Level of Comprehension

___—___ 1. Where did the story take place?
(I. B. Belcher Elementary School or at a school)

setting/literal
I don't remember.

___+___ 2. Who were the two main characters in the story?
(Jamie Lee and Josh Kidder)

character-characterization/ literal Josh and Jamie

___+___ 3. What was the problem between Jamie and Josh?
(Jamie didn't think Josh could be a good player because of his shoes, Josh didn't fit in, or other plausible response)

story problem(s)/inferential
Jamie didn't like Josh because he had old shoes and was different.

___—___ 4. How did Josh solve his problem with the other boys?
(he outplayed all of them)

problem resolution/ inferential
He ignored them.

___—___ 5. What kind of person was Jamie Lee?
(conceited, stuck-up, or other plausible responses)

character-characterization/ evaluative
tall ... a big tall boy

___+___ 6. What happened after the game?
(the other boys gathered around and asked Josh his secret)

problem resolution attempts/ literal Everyone wanted to know how Josh learned to play so good.

___+___ 7. Why did everyone laugh when Josh said, "Two things—lots of practice and cheap shoes"?
(because everything had happened because of his cheap shoes)

problem resolution attempts/ inferential It was funny. Because he played good even with lousy shoes.

___—___ 8. What lesson does this story teach?
(responses will vary but should indicate a theme/moral related to "it's not what you wear that makes you good in a sport")

theme/evaluative
Josh was better than Jamie.

PART II: ORAL READING AND ANALYSIS OF MISCUES

Directions: Say, "Now I would like to hear you read this story out loud." Have the student read orally until the 100-word sample is completed. Follow along on the Miscue Grid, marking any oral reading errors as appropriate. *Remember to count miscues only up to the point in the story containing the oral reading stop-marker (//).* Then complete the Developmental/Performance Summary to determine whether to continue the assessment. (*Note:* The Miscue Grid should be completed *after* the assessment session has been concluded in order to minimize stress for the student.)

	MIS-PRONUN.	SUB-STITUTION	OMISSION	INSERTION	TCHR. ASSIST.	SELF-CORRECT.	MEANING DISRUPTION
Hot Shoes							
The guys at (the) I. B. Belcher							
Elementary School ~~loved~~ lived (SC) all the							
new sport shoes. Some ~~wore~~ wib the							
"Sky High" model by Leader.							
Others who really couldn't afford buy Sky							
Highs would settle for a lesser							
shoe. Some liked have the "Street							
Smarts" by Master, or (the)							
"Uptown-Downtown s" by Beebop.							
The Belcher boys got get to the point							
with their shoes that they could							
impea identify their friends just by							
looking at their feet shoes (SC). But the boy							
who was the envy every of the entire fifth							
grade was Jamie Lee. He had a							
pair of "High Five Pump 'em Ups"							
by Superior. The only thing Belcher							
boys loved as // much as their							
shoes was basketball.							
TOTALS							

Notes:

The total number of miscues is 12, not counting the 2 self-corrections.

Examiner's Summary of Miscue Patterns:

The student had several repetitions and substitutions.
This might indicate he is using context to search for meaning.

PART III: DEVELOPMENTAL/PERFORMANCE SUMMARY

Silent Reading Comprehension		**Oral Reading Accuracy**	
_____	0–1 questions missed = Easy	_____	0–1 oral errors = Easy
_____	2 questions missed = Adequate	_____	2–5 oral errors = Adequate
✔	3+ questions missed = Too hard	✔	6+ oral errors = Too hard

Continue to next assessment level passage?   _____ Yes   ✔ No

Examiner's Notes:

Very tough passage. Unaided recall was limited and he only included the characters and the story problem. He couldn't remember very much of the story. Every question required probing. He doesn't seem to understand the concept of "theme."

STUDENT SUMMARY

Student's Name: _Frank Zevon_

Examiner: _____ Date: _____

Form(s) Used: (A)   B   C   D

PERFORMANCE LEVELS ON SENTENCES
FOR INITIAL PASSAGE SELECTION

_____ _____ Highest level with zero (0) errors

_____ _____ First level with two (2) or more errors

OVERALL PERFORMANCE ON READING PASSAGES

_____ _____ Easy reading level (independent)

_____ _____ Adequate reading level (instructional)

_____ _____ Too hard reading level (frustration)

MISCUE SUMMARY
COMPREHENSION RESPONSE SUMMARY CHART

	MISPRONUNCIATION	SUBSTITUTION	INSERTION	TEACHER ASSISTANCE	OMISSION	TOTALS
TOTALS	2	6	2	0	2	12
SELF-CORRECTION	0	2	0	0	0	2
MEANING DISRUPTIONS	2	2	0	0	0	4

Narrative Passages (Forms A and B)

STORY GRAMMAR ELEMENT	UNAIDED RECALL	AIDED RECALL	NUMBER NOT RECALLED	% RECALLED
CHARACTER CHARACTERIZATION	1	—	1	50
SETTING	—	—	1	0
STORY PROBLEM	1	—	—	100
PROBLEM RESOLUTION ATTEMPT	—	2	—	100
RESOLUTION	—	—	1	0
THEME/MORAL	—	—	1	0

Expository Passages (Forms C and D)

EXPOSITORY GRAMMAR ELEMENT	UNAIDED RECALL	AIDED RECALL	NUMBER NOT RECALLED	% RECALLED
COLLECTIVE				
CAUSATIVE				
DESCRIPTIVE				
COMPARISON				
PROBLEM RESOLUTION				

SUMMARY TABLE OF PERCENTAGES

PASSAGE LEVEL	SILENT READING COMPREHENSION	ORAL READING ACCURACY
1		
2		
3		
4		
5	50% 4/8	90%
6		
7		
8		
9		
10		
11		
12		

THE FLYNT-COOTER READING INVENTORY

STUDENT SUMMARY

Student's Name: _____

Examiner: _____ Date: _____

Form(s) Used: A   B   C   D

PERFORMANCE LEVELS ON SENTENCES FOR INITIAL PASSAGE SELECTION

_____   Highest level with zero (0) errors

_____   First level with two (2) or more errors

OVERALL PERFORMANCE ON READING PASSAGES

_____   Easy reading level (independent)

_____   Adequate reading level (instructional)

_____   Too hard reading level (frustration)

MISCUE SUMMARY
COMPREHENSION RESPONSE SUMMARY CHART

	MISPRONUNCIATION	SUBSTITUTION	INSERTION	TEACHER ASSISTANCE	OMISSION	TOTALS
TOTALS						
SELF-CORRECTION						
MEANING DISRUPTIONS						

Narrative Passages (Forms A and B)

STORY GRAMMAR ELEMENT	UNAIDED RECALL	AIDED RECALL	NUMBER NOT RECALLED	% RECALLED
CHARACTER CHARACTERIZATION				
SETTING				
STORY PROBLEM				
PROBLEM RESOLUTION ATTEMPT				
PROBLEM RESOLUTION				
THEME/MORAL				

Expository Passages (Forms C and D)

EXPOSITORY GRAMMAR ELEMENT	UNAIDED RECALL	AIDED RECALL	NUMBER NOT RECALLED	% RECALLED
COLLECTIVE				
CAUSATIVE				
DESCRIPTIVE				
COMPARISON				
PROBLEM RESOLUTION				

SUMMARY TABLE OF PERCENTAGES

PASSAGE LEVEL	SILENT READING COMPREHENSION	ORAL READING ACCURACY
1		
2		
3		
4		
5		
6		
7		
8		
9		
10		
11		
12		

Briefly describe what you discovered about the student in the Interest/Attitude Interview.

ORAL READING SKILLS

Directions: Place an **X** by the characteristic(s) evident during this assessment.

_____ Reads in phrases (not word by word)		_____ Word-by-word reader
_____ Reads with expression		_____ Reads with little expression
_____ Attends to punctuation		_____ Ignores punctuation
_____ Uses word identification strategies		_____ Weak word identification ability
_____ Has few repetitions		_____ Has lots of repetitions

SUMMARY OF ABILITIES AND NEEDS IN *ORAL READING*

SUMMARY OF ABILITIES AND NEEDS IN *READING COMPREHENSION*

Directions: Include all information related to retellings, question/story grammar types, and use of comprehension strategies.

FIRST INTERVENTION STRATEGIES

Directions: Describe any intervention/teaching strategies you feel should be tried initially. These strategies should help you learn more about the student's reading abilities and confirm or reject findings drawn from this inventory and should also help the student continue to grow as a successful reader.

⬛ INTEREST/ATTITUDE INTERVIEW ⬛

PRIMARY FORM

Student's Name: _____ Age: _____

Date: _____ Examiner: _____

Introductory Statement: [*Student's name*], *before you read some stories for me I would like to ask you some questions.*

Home Life

1. Where do you live? Do you know your address? What is it?

2. Who lives in your house with you?

3. What kinds of jobs do you have at home?

4. What is one thing that you really like to do at home?

5. Do you ever read at home? [*If yes, ask:*] When do you read and what was the last thing you read? [*If no, ask:*] Does anyone ever read to you? [*If so, ask:*] Who, and how often?

6. Do you have a bedtime on school nights? [*If no, ask:*] When do you go to bed?

7. Do you have a TV in your room? How much TV do you watch every day? What are your favorite shows?

8. What do you like to do with your friends?

9. Do you have any pets? Do you collect things? Do you take any kinds of lessons?

10. When you make a new friend, what is something that your friend ought to know about you?

School Life

1. Besides recess and lunch, what do you like about school?

2. Do you get to read much in school?

3. Are you a good reader or a not-so-good reader?

   [*If a good reader, ask:*] What makes a person a good reader?

   [*If a not-so-good reader, ask:*] What causes a person to not be a good reader?

4. If you could pick any book to read, what would the book be about?

5. Do you like to write? What kind of writing do you do in school? What is the favorite thing you have written about?

6. Who has helped you the most in school? How did that person help you?

7. Do you have a place at home to study?

8. Do you get help with your homework? Who helps you?

9. What was the last book you read for school?

10. If you were helping someone learn to read, what could you do to help that person?

▄▄▃ INTEREST/ATTITUDE INTERVIEW ▃▄▄

UPPER LEVEL FORM

Student's Name: _____ Age: _____

Date: _____ Examiner: _____

Introductory Statement: [*Student's name*], *before you read some stories for me I would like to ask you some questions.*

Home Life

1. How many people are there in your family?

2. Do you have your own room or do you share a room? [*Ask this only if it is apparent that the student has siblings.*]

3. Do your parent(s) work? What kinds of jobs do they have?

4. Do you have jobs around the house? What are they?

5. What do you usually do after school?

6. Do you have a TV in your room? How much time do you spend watching TV each day? What are your favorite shows?

7. Do you have a bedtime during the week? What time do you usually go to bed on a school night?

8. Do you get an allowance? How much?

9. Do you belong to any clubs at school or outside school? What are they?

10. What are some things that you really like to do? Do you collect things, have any hobbies, or take lessons outside school?

School Environment

1. Do you like school? What is your favorite class? Your least favorite class?

2. Do you have a special place to study at home?

3. How much homework do you have on a typical school night? Does anyone help you with your homework? Who?

4. Do you consider yourself a good reader or a not-so-good reader?

   [*If a good reader, ask:*] What has helped you most to become a good reader?

   [*If a not-so-good reader, ask:*] What causes someone to be a not-so-good reader?

5. If I gave you the choice of selecting a book about any topic, what would you choose to read about?

6. What is one thing you can think of that would help you become a better reader? Is there anything else?

7. Do you like to write? What kind of writing assignments do you like best?

8. If you went to a new school, what is one thing that you would want the teachers to know about you as a student?

9. If you were helping someone learn to read, what would be the most important thing you could do to help that person?

10. How will knowing how to read help you in the future?

FORM A

Sentences for Initial Passage Selection

FORM A: LEVEL 1

1. He wanted to fly.

2. The family got together.

3. The boy was jumping.

FORM A: LEVEL 2

1. I was walking fast to town.

2. She cried about going home.

3. I was pulled out of the hole.

FORM A: LEVEL 3

1. The forest was something to see.

2. I was enjoying sleeping when my Mom called.

3. I had to go to bed early last night.

FORM A: LEVEL 4

1. I thought the lunches were terrible.

2. Chocolate is my favorite thing to eat.

3. Everything was quiet after the contest.

FORM A: LEVEL 5

1. Athletic shoes come in all kinds of colors.

2. Serious players manage to practice a lot.

3. A cheap pair of shoes doesn't last very long.

FORM A: LEVEL 6

1. He was searching for the evidence.

2. She realized the rock formations were too high.

3. The conservationist hoped to reforest the mountain.

FORM A: LEVEL 7

1. Unfortunately she was confused about the next activity.

2. The submerged rocks were dangerous.

3. She disappeared around the bend at a rapid rate.

FORM A: LEVEL 8

1. Ascending the mountain was rigorous and hazardous.

2. The cliff provided a panoramic view of the valley.

3. The incubation period lasted two weeks.

FORM A: LEVEL 9

1. The abduction made everyone suspicious.

2. The detective was besieged by the community.

3. Her pasty complexion made her look older.

FORM A
Narrative Passages

1

I went swimming.

2

My dog jumped in the pool.

3

My friends came over and jumped in the pool too.

4

We had a great time swimming.

You Cannot Fly!

Once a boy named Sam wanted to fly.

His mother and father said, "You cannot fly."

His sister said, "You cannot fly."

Sam tried jumping off a box.

He tried jumping off his bed.

He fell down each time.

Sam still tried hard but he still could not fly.

Then one day a letter came for Sam.

The letter said, "Come and see me, Sam, on the next airplane."

It was from his grandfather.

Sam went to his family and read the letter.

Sam said, "Now I can fly."

Sam and his family all laughed together.

The Pig and the Snake

One day Mr. Pig was walking to town.

He saw a big hole in the road.

A big snake was in the hole.

"Help me," said the snake, "and I will be your friend."

"No, no," said Mr. Pig. "If I help you get out you will bite me. You are a snake!"

The snake cried and cried.

So Mr. Pig pulled the snake out of the hole.

Then the snake said, "Now I am going to bite you, Mr. Pig."

"How can you bite me after I helped you out of the hole?" said Mr. Pig.

The snake said, "You knew I was a snake when you pulled me out!"

The Big Bad Wolf

One day Mr. Wolf was walking through the forest. He was enjoying an afternoon walk and not bothering anyone. All of a sudden it started to rain and he became wet and cold.

Just when Mr. Wolf was about to freeze to death, he saw a small house in the woods. Smoke was coming from the chimney, so he knocked on the door. No one was home, but a note on the door said:

Come in and make yourself warm. I'll be back about 2:00 p.m.

Love,

Granny

The poor wet wolf came in and began to warm himself by the fire. He saw one of Granny's nightgowns on the bed, so he decided to put it on instead of his wet clothes. Since he was still very, very cold he decided to get into Granny's bed. Soon he was fast asleep.

Mr. Wolf fell into a deep sleep. When he awoke, Mr. Wolf found an old woman, a little girl wearing a red coat, and a woodcutter standing around the bed. The woodcutter was yelling at Mr. Wolf and saying something about how he was going to kill him with his axe. Mr. Wolf jumped out of the bed and ran for his life.

Later that day, Mr. Wolf was finally safe at home. His wife said, "Just you wait, those humans will make up a story about how big and bad *you* were."

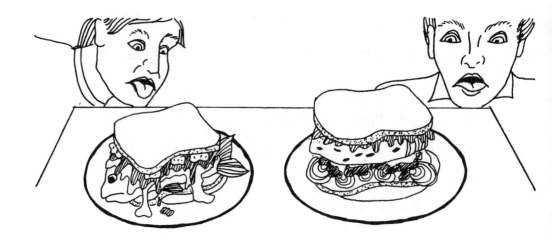

The Terrible Lunch Contest

Jason and Chris didn't like the lunches at their school. They thought anything would taste better than the soybean hamburgers they had every Wednesday. They also didn't like the cardboard-tasting pizza on Fridays.

One day Chris said, "Wouldn't it be funny if we had a terrible lunch contest? You know, we could see who could bring a lunch that is worse than the lunchroom food." Jason said, "OK, but the winner has to eat whatever he brings. The loser has to buy the winner a candy bar." The contest was on.

The very next Wednesday the boys were ready. Jason brought a sandwich made with fish, marshmallow cream, chocolate sauce, pickles, and ketchup. He called it his "something's fishy" sandwich. But Chris seemed to have him beaten. His sandwich was made with two pieces of onion, cooked chicken livers, a slice of watermelon, sour cream, peanut butter, and beans. Chris called his the "chicken delight!"

Everyone gathered around to see who would win. Even Mrs. Smith, the lunchroom lady, came to watch. "Who's the winner?" she asked. "Whoever eats his sandwich wins," said Kelly, a girl in their class. Then everything was quiet.

The two boys looked at their terrible sandwiches. Then they looked at each other. Jason looked at Mrs. Smith and said, "I think you win. I sure would like to have one of your hamburgers instead of this mess." Chris quickly agreed. After that both boys were happy to eat hamburgers on Wednesday and pizza on Friday.

Hot Shoes

The guys at the I. B. Belcher Elementary School loved all the new sport shoes. Some wore the "Sky High" model by Leader. Others who couldn't afford Sky Highs would settle for a lesser shoe. Some liked the "Street Smarts" by Master, or the "Uptown-Downtown" by Beebop. The Belcher boys got to the point with their shoes that they could identify their friends just by looking at their feet. But the boy who was the envy of the entire fifth grade was Jamie Lee. He had a pair of "High Five Pump 'em Ups" by Superior. The only thing Belcher boys loved as much as their shoes was basketball. They would lace up their fancy athletic shoes and play basketball all afternoon. Everyone was sure that the shoes helped them jump higher and run faster.

One day a new student showed up on the playground. His name was Josh Kidder, and no one knew him. He lived in the poor part of town and wore a cheap pair of black hightop tennis shoes. They were made by an old fashioned company called White Dot. When Jamie Lee saw Josh's White Dot shoes, he said, "No serious basketball player wears White Dots. Where have you been, Kidder?" Josh said, "Well, I may not have a pair of shoes like yours but I would like to play basketball with you and the other guys."

Jamie Lee and the other boys kind of chuckled and said, "Sure kid, no problem." What happened next is a matter of history now at I. B. Belcher School. Josh ran faster, jumped higher, and scored more points (35 points to be exact) than anybody else that day. Jamie Lee, whom Josh guarded, only managed two points.

When it was all over the boys gathered around Josh. He was the hero of the day. "What's your secret weapon?" asked Randy. Josh just smiled and said, "Two things—lots of practice and cheap shoes." Everyone laughed.

Mountain Fire

One August afternoon Brad and Kevin went tracking with their fathers on Mount Holyoak. Brad's father was a conservationist for the Forest Service and was searching for evidence of cougars. Many people feared that the cougars were extinct on Mount Holyoak. The boys became excited when they found what appeared to be a partial cougar track near a stream. But as the day wore on, no new tracks were found.

After lunch Brad's father sent the boys upstream while he circled west. He told the boys to return to the lunch site in an hour. After about forty-five minutes, the boys found the stream's source and could follow it no more. They decided to search close to the stream before starting back. They saw interesting rock formations, eagles' nests on high ledges and, finally, two fresh cougar footprints. Both boys were very excited until they realized that they no longer could hear the stream. They were lost.

The boys searched an hour or more for the mountain stream, but without success. They were tired, dirty, and getting worried. Brad decided to start a small fire in hopes of his father seeing the smoke. Kevin reminded Brad of the danger of forest fires but finally agreed to help collect the twigs, branches, and brush. The moment Brad struck a match in the extra-dry mountain air and stuck it to the dry tinder, the fire exploded into a large fireball.

In a matter of minutes, trees all around the boys burst into flames. The fire spread quickly up the mountainside. The boys ran downhill as fast as they could.

Before the day was out, hotshot crews, airplanes carrying fire retardants, and bucket-loaded helicopters were on the scene trying to contain the fire. The fire raged for days, however, and by the time it was put out over 45,000 acres of timber had been consumed.

For several years Brad and Kevin spent every spare moment helping to reforest the mountain. One day the forest ranger commented, "Well, boys, it looks like things are about back to normal." Brad looked down at his feet and sadly replied, "Maybe, but no new cougar tracks have been seen since the fire."

The Canoe Trip

Katherine and her family like to spend their vacation camping out. Frequently they go to either Great Smoky Mountains National Park or Yellowstone National Park. Since they have camped out for many years, they have become quite accomplished. Katherine is able to start a fire with flint and steel, build a lean-to for shelter, and find food in the forest on which to live.

Katherine's favorite outdoor activity is canoeing. Although she is quite a good canoer, there is one canoe trip that she'll never forget. It was a canoe trip she took with her family and her friend Amy down the Madison River near West Yellowstone.

Katherine and Amy were in a canoe together following her parents down the river. The early going was fine and they didn't have any major problems. The girls did get confused once or twice in their steering and the boat would go sideways. But after about thirty minutes on the river, Katherine and Amy felt secure about their ability to navigate. Unfortunately their canoe could not keep up with Katherine's parents' canoe because they were carrying all the rations in two coolers. Slowly the lead canoe disappeared around a bend.

When the girls' canoe rounded a bend, not only could they not see the lead canoe but they were heading directly into some rough white water. The rough water was swift and there were a lot of rocks submerged below the surface. The swiftness and rocks were causing problems for the jittery canoe and the two inexperienced girls.

Just as the canoe was about to clear the rough water it struck a large boulder just beneath the surface. Before the girls knew what had happened the canoe had capsized, sending them into the icy cold river. Naturally they had on life jackets so they were not in much danger. But the two coolers full of food and the canoe started floating away from them at a rapid rate.

Katherine managed to grab hold of the canoe and one paddle. Amy swam over to the shore. After much effort both girls managed to pull in the canoe, empty the water, and start downstream after the lost coolers. But since they had only one paddle they limped along, unable to catch up to the now disappeared coolers.

Some forty-five minutes later, feeling cold and upset, the girls rounded a sharp bend in the river. To their surprise they saw the rest of the family sitting on the south-side shore of the river. Katherine's Dad had built a fire and was roasting hot dogs. Katherine's mother and little brother were sitting on the two coolers eating a hot dog and munching on potato chips. Dad said, "What took you two so long? We didn't know you were going to stop and take a swim, but thanks for sending the food on ahead." As cold as they were Katherine and Amy couldn't help but laugh.

The Eagle

There exists an old Native American legend about an eagle who thought he was a chicken. It seems that a Hopi farmer and his only son decided to climb a nearby mountain to observe an eagle's nest. The trip would take them all day, so they brought along some rations and water for the trek. The man and the boy crossed the enormous fields of maize and beans into the foothills. Soon thereafter they were ascending the mountain and the climb became rigorous and hazardous. They occasionally looked back toward their home and at the panoramic view of the entire valley.

Finally the farmer and son reached the mountain's summit. Perched on the highest point on a ledge was the eagle's nest. The farmer reached his hand into the nest after realizing that the mother had gone in search of food. He brought out a most precious prize, an eagle's egg. He tucked it into his tunic and the two descended the mount.

The egg was placed in the nest of a chicken for incubation. It soon hatched. The eaglet grew with the baby chicks and adopted their habits for gathering food in the barnyard; namely, scratching for feed the farmer threw out.

Some time later an Anasazi brave passed through the area and saw this enormous brown eagle scratching and walking about in the barnyard. He dismounted from his horse and went to the farmer. "Why do you have an eagle acting as a chicken? It is not right," queried the noble brave.

"That's no eagle, it's a chicken," retorted the farmer. "Can't you see that it scratches for food with the other chickens? No, it is indeed a chicken," exclaimed the farmer.

"I will show you that this is an eagle," said the brave.

The brave took the eagle on his arm and climbed to the top of the barn. Then saying, "You are an eagle, the most noble of birds. Fly and soar as you were destined!" He threw the eagle from the barn. But the startled eagle fluttered to the ground and began pecking for food.

"See," said the farmer. "I told you it is a chicken."

The brave replied, "I'll show you this is an eagle. It is clear what I must do."

Again the brave took the eagle on his arm and began walking toward the mountain. He climbed all day until he reached a high bluff overlooking the valley. Then the brave, with outstretched arm, held the bird out and said, "You are an eagle, the most noble of birds. Fly and soar as you were destined to."

Just then a mountain breeze washed across the eagle. His eyes brightened as he caught the wild scent of freedom. In a moment the eagle stretched his mighty wings and let out a magnificent screech. Leaping from the brave's arm, he flew high into the western sky.

The eagle saw more of the world in that one great moment than his barnyard friends would discover in a lifetime.

The Case of Angela Violet

Angela Violet was an elderly lady in our neighborhood who some people thought suspicious. She was rarely seen outside her spacious Victorian-styled home, and then only to retrieve the daily mail. Her pasty complexion and ancient dress made her appear like an apparition. Small children in the neighborhood speculated that she might be some sort of witch. It appeared that Miss Violet had no contact with the outside world.

One autumn day news spread through the community that a high school cheerleader, Katrina Bowers, had disappeared. It was feared by the police that Katrina had been abducted. State and local police joined forces with the Federal Bureau of Investigation in the massive search effort. In spite of all the best efforts of the constabulary, no trace of Katrina Bowers was uncovered. After ten days of suspense and worry, the search was called off.

Three weeks after Katrina's apparent abduction a break in the case occurred. An anonymous telephone caller informed the police that Miss Angela Violet had kidnapped Katrina. It was alleged that Miss Violet was holding her captive in her basement. Because of Miss Violet's unusual lifestyle, the police were inclined to give some credence to the tip. A search warrant was issued and the police converged on her house.

Detective Donna Jordan knocked on the shabby door of Miss Violet's residence. Two other officers attended Detective Jordan. Miss Violet showed surprise, but welcomed the police into her home graciously. She consented to having her home searched.

By the time the police had completed their search, two television news trucks had taken position outside her home. When the detectives came out of the house without Miss Violet, the anxious newsmen besieged them with queries.

Detective Jordan stepped forward and calmly said, "What we found was a kindly lady who is caring night and day for her ailing mother. There is no evidence whatsoever that Miss Violet has any involvement in the Katrina Bowers case."

People in the community began to reach out to Miss Violet and her mother from then on. They took food and sat with Miss Violet's mother so she could get out more. As for Katrina Bowers, she was located safe and sound in California with relatives. She had been a runaway case.

FORM A

Examiner's Assessment Protocols

FORM A: PREPRIMER (PP) LEVEL ASSESSMENT PROTOCOLS

The Accident (Wordless picture story)

PART I: WORDLESS PICTURE STORY READING

Background Statement: "These pictures tell a story about a girl and something that happened to her. Look at each picture as I show it to you and think about the story the pictures tell. Later, I will want you to tell me the story using the pictures."

Teacher Directions: Refer the student to each picture slowly and in order as numbered. Do not comment on the pictures. Then repeat the procedure, asking the student to tell the story in the student's own words. Record the student's reading using a tape recorder, and transcribe the reading as it is being dictated. Replay the recording later to make sure that your transcription is accurate and complete.

PART II: EMERGENT READING BEHAVIOR CHECKLIST

Directions: Following are emergent reading behaviors identified through research and grouped according to broad developmental stages. Check all behaviors you have observed. *If the student progresses to Stage 3 or 4, continue your assessment using the Primer Level (P) passage.*

Stage 1: Early Connections to Reading—Describing Pictures

_____ Attends to and describes (labels) pictures in books

_____ Has a limited sense of story

_____ Follows verbal directions for this activity

_____ Uses oral vocabulary appropriate for age/grade level

_____ Displays attention span appropriate for age/grade level

_____ Responds to questions in an appropriate manner

_____ Appears to connect pictures (sees as being interrelated)

Stage 2: Connecting Pictures to Form Story

_____ Attends to pictures and develops oral stories across the pages of the book

_____ Uses only childlike or descriptive (storyteller) language to tell the story, rather than book language (i.e., Once upon a time...; There once was a little boy...)

Stage 3: Transitional Picture Reading

_____ Attends to pictures as a connected story

_____ Mixes storyteller language with book language

Stage 4: Advanced Picture Reading

_____   Attends to pictures and develops oral stories across the pages of the book

_____   Speaks as though reading the story (uses book language)

Examiner's Notes:

FORM A: PRIMER (P) LEVEL ASSESSMENT PROTOCOLS

Let's Go Swimming (25 words)

PART I: PICTURE STORY READING—ORAL READING AND ANALYSIS OF MISCUES

Background Statement: "This is a story about a child having fun. Let's look at each picture first. Now, read the story to yourself. Later, I will want you to read the story to me."

Teacher Directions: Refer the student to each frame of the story slowly and in order as numbered. Do not read the story or comment on the pictures. After the student has read the story silently, ask the student to read the story aloud. Record the student's reading using a tape recorder, and mark any miscues on the Miscue Grid provided. Following the oral reading, complete the Emergent Reading Behavior Checklist. Assessment information obtained from both the Miscue Grid and the Emergent Reading Behavior Checklist will help you determine whether to continue your assessment. If the student is unable to read the passage independently the first time, read it aloud, then ask the student to try to read the story again. This will help you understand whether the student is able to memorize and repeat text, an important developmental milestone (see the *Instructions for Administering the Preprimer (PP) and Primer (P) Passages* section in the front of this book for more information). The assessment should stop after this activity, if the child is unable to read the text independently. (*Note:* The Miscue Grid should be completed *after* the assessment session has been concluded in order to minimize stress for the student.)

	MIS-PRONUN.	SUB-STITUTION	OMISSION	INSERTION	TCHR. ASSIST.	SELF-CORRECT.	MEANING DISRUPTION
Let's Go Swimming							
I went swimming.							
My dog jumped in the							
pool. My friends came							
over and jumped in							
the pool too. We had							
a great time swimming.							
TOTALS							

Notes:

PART II: EMERGENT READING BEHAVIOR CHECKLIST

Directions: Following are emergent reading behaviors identified through research and grouped according to broad developmental stages. After the student has completed the oral reading, check each behavior observed below to help determine development level and whether to continue the assessment. *If the student seems to be at Stage 6 or 7 and the oral reading scored at an Easy or Adequate level, continue the assessment using the Level 1 passage.*

Stage 5: Early Print Reading

_____ Tells a story using the pictures

_____ Knows print moves from left to right, top to bottom

_____ Creates part of the text using book language and knows some words on sight

Stage 6: Early Strategic Reading

_____ Uses context to guess at some unknown words (guesses make sense)

_____ Notices beginning sounds in words and uses them in guessing unknown words

_____ Seems to sometimes use syntax to help identify words in print

_____ Recognizes some word parts, such as root words and affixes

Stage 7: Moderate Strategic Reading

_____ Sometimes uses context and word parts to decode words

_____ Self-corrects when making an oral reading miscue

_____ Retells the passage easily and may embellish the storyline

_____ Shows some awareness of vowel sounds

Examiner's Notes:

Examiner's Summary of Miscue Patterns:

PART III: DEVELOPMENTAL/PERFORMANCE SUMMARY

Oral Reading Accuracy

_____   0–1   oral errors = Easy

_____   2–5   oral errors = Adequate

_____   6+   oral errors = Too hard

Continue to next assessment level passage? _____ Yes _____ No

Examiner's Notes:

FORM A: LEVEL 1 ASSESSMENT PROTOCOLS

You Cannot Fly! (96 words)

PART I: SILENT READING COMPREHENSION

Background Statement: "Have you ever wished you could fly? A boy named Sam in this story wants to fly. Read this story to find out if Sam gets to fly. Read it carefully because when you're through I'm going to ask you to tell me about the story."

Teacher Directions: Once the student completes the silent reading, say, "Tell me about the story you just read." Check off any answers to the questions below that the student provides during the retelling. Ask all remaining questions not addressed during the retelling.

Questions/Answers	*Story Grammar Element/ Level of Comprehension*
_____1. What was the name of the boy in the story? *(Sam)*	character-characterization/ literal
_____2. What did Sam really want to do? *(Sam wanted to fly, but couldn't)*	story problem(s)/literal
_____3. What were two ways Sam tried to fly? *(jumping off his bed and a box)*	problem resolution attempts/ literal
_____4. How was Sam's problem finally solved? *(Sam got to ride on an airplane)*	problem resolution/ inferential
_____5. What did the family and Sam do after reading the letter? *(laughed)*	problem resolution attempts/ literal
_____6. Where did the story take place? *(Sam's house)*	setting/inferential
_____7. What did Sam learn about being able to fly? *(people can't fly except in airplanes)*	theme/evaluative
_____8. What words would you use to tell someone what kind of boy Sam was? *(responses will vary; accept plausible ones)*	character-characterization/ evaluative

PART II: ORAL READING AND ANALYSIS OF MISCUES

Directions: Say, "Now I would like to hear you read this story out loud. Please start at the beginning and keep reading until I tell you to stop." Have the student read orally until the oral reading stop-marker (//) is reached. Follow along on the Miscue Grid, marking any oral reading errors as appropriate. Then complete the Developmental/Performance Summary to determine whether to continue the assessment. (*Note:* The Miscue Grid should be completed *after* the assessment session has been concluded in order to minimize stress for the student.)

	MIS-PRONUN.	SUB-STITUTION	OMISSION	INSERTION	TCHR. ASSIST.	SELF-CORRECT.	MEANING DISRUPTION
You Cannot Fly!							
Once a boy named Sam wanted to							
fly. His mother and father said,							
"You cannot fly." His sister said,							
"You cannot fly." Sam tried jumping							
off a box. He tried jumping off							
his bed. He fell down each time.							
Sam still tried hard but he still							
could not fly. Then one day							
a letter came for Sam. The letter							
said, "Come and see me, Sam, on							
the next airplane." It was from							
his grandfather. Sam went to his							
family and read the letter. Sam							
said, "Now I can fly." Sam and his							
family all laughed together. //							
TOTALS							

Notes:

Examiner's Summary of Miscue Patterns:

PART III: DEVELOPMENTAL/PERFORMANCE SUMMARY

Silent Reading Comprehension   *Oral Reading Accuracy*

_____ 0–1 questions missed = Easy   _____ 0–1 oral errors = Easy

_____ 2   questions missed = Adequate   _____ 2–5 oral errors = Adequate

_____ 3+   questions missed = Too hard   _____ 6+   oral errors = Too hard

Continue to next assessment level passage?   _____ Yes   _____ No

Examiner's Notes:

FORM A: LEVEL 2 ASSESSMENT PROTOCOLS

The Pig and the Snake (111 words)

PART I: SILENT READING COMPREHENSION

Background Statement: "Read this story to find out what happened to Mr. Pig when he tried to help a snake in trouble. Be sure and read it carefully because I'm going to ask you to tell me about the story."

Teacher Directions: Once the student completes the silent reading, say, "Tell me about the story you just read." Check off any answers to the questions below that the student provides during the retelling. Ask all remaining questions not addressed during the retelling.

Questions/Answers	*Story Grammar Element/ Level of Comprehension*
_____1. Where did the story take place? *(on the road to town)*	setting/literal
_____2. Who were the animals in the story? *(Mr. Pig and a snake)*	character-characterization/ literal
_____3. What was the snake's problem? *(he was stuck in a hole and wanted help getting out)*	story problem(s)/literal
_____4. How did the snake solve his problem? *(by getting the pig to help him by promising not to hurt him)*	problem resolution/ inferential
_____5. What words would you use to describe the snake? *(sneaky, liar, or any other plausible response)*	character-characterization/ evaluative
_____6. What lesson did Mr. Pig learn? *(responses will vary but should indicate a theme/moral related to "you can't always trust what someone says")*	theme/evaluative
_____7. How did Mr. Pig feel after he helped pull the snake out of the hole? *(surprised, upset, etc.)*	character-characterization/ inferential
_____8. What was one thing the snake did to get Mr. Pig to help him out of the hole? *(cried or said he would be his friend)*	problem resolution attempts/ literal

PART II: ORAL READING AND ANALYSIS OF MISCUES

Directions: Say, "Now I would like to hear you read this story out loud." Have the student read orally until the 100-word sample is completed. Follow along on the Miscue Grid, marking any oral reading errors as appropriate. *Remember to count miscues only up to the point in the story containing the oral reading stop-marker (//).* Then complete the Developmental/Performance Summary to determine whether to continue the assessment. (*Note:* The Miscue Grid should be completed *after* the assessment session has been concluded in order to minimize stress for the student.)

	MIS-PRONUN.	SUB-STITUTION	OMISSION	INSERTION	TCHR. ASSIST.	SELF-CORRECT.	MEANING DISRUPTION
The Pig and the Snake							
One day Mr. Pig was walking to							
town. He saw a big hole in the							
road. A big snake was in the							
hole. "Help me," said the snake,							
"and I will be your friend." "No, no,"							
said Mr. Pig. "If I help you get							
out you will bite me. You are							
a snake!" The snake cried and							
cried. So Mr. Pig pulled the							
snake out of the hole.							
Then the snake said, "Now I am							
going to bite you, Mr. Pig."							
"How can you bite me after							
I helped you out of the hole?"							
said Mr. Pig. The snake said, //							
"You knew I was a snake							
when you pulled me out!"							
TOTALS							

Notes:

Examiner's Summary of Miscue Patterns:

PART III: DEVELOPMENTAL/PERFORMANCE SUMMARY

Silent Reading Comprehension

_____ 0–1 questions missed = Easy

_____ 2   questions missed = Adequate

_____ 3+   questions missed = Too hard

Oral Reading Accuracy

_____ 0–1 oral errors = Easy

_____ 2–5 oral errors = Adequate

_____ 6+   oral errors = Too hard

Continue to next assessment level passage?   _____ Yes   _____ No

Examiner's Notes:

The Big Bad Wolf (235 words)

PART I: SILENT READING COMPREHENSION

Background Statement: "Have you ever had someone say something about you that wasn't true? Mr. Wolf thinks he has. Read and find out what really happened. Read it carefully because I'm going to ask you to tell me about the story."

Teacher Directions: Once the student completes the silent reading, say, "Tell me about the story you just read." Check off any answers to the questions below that the student provides during the retelling. Ask all remaining questions not addressed during the retelling.

Questions/Answers	*Story Grammar Element/ Level of Comprehension*
_____1. Who was the story about? *(Mr. Wolf, Granny, little girl, woodcutter)*	character-characterization/ literal
_____2. Where was Mr. Wolf when he saw the house? *(in the forest)*	setting/literal
_____3. Why did Mr. Wolf need to get into the house? *(he was wet and freezing)*	story problem(s)/literal
_____4. What made Mr. Wolf think it was OK to go into the house? *(the note on the door)*	problem resolution attempts/ inferential
_____5. What did Mr. Wolf do after entering the house? *(began to warm himself and changed into a nightgown)*	problem resolution attempts/ literal
_____6. Why did Mr. Wolf have to run for his life? *(woodcutter was going to kill him)*	problem resolution attempts/ literal
_____7. What lesson did Mr. Wolf learn? *(responses will vary but should indicate a theme/moral related to not doing things without permission)*	theme/evaluative
_____8. What did Mrs. Wolf say that would make you think she didn't trust humans? *(she said the humans would make up a story about her husband)*	character-characterization/ inferential

PART II: ORAL READING AND ANALYSIS OF MISCUES

Directions: Say, "Now I would like to hear you read this story out loud." Have the student read orally until the 100-word sample is completed. Follow along on the Miscue Grid, marking any oral reading errors as appropriate. *Remember to count miscues only up to the point in the story containing the oral reading stop-marker (//).* Then complete the Developmental/Performance Summary to determine whether to continue the assessment. (*Note:* The Miscue Grid should be completed *after* the assessment session has been concluded in order to minimize stress for the student.)

	MIS-PRONUN.	SUB-STITUTION	OMISSION	INSERTION	TCHR. ASSIST.	SELF-CORRECT.	MEANING DISRUPTION
The Big Bad Wolf							
One day Mr. Wolf was walking							
through the forest. He was enjoying							
an afternoon walk and not bothering							
anyone. All of a sudden it started							
to rain and he became wet and cold.							
Just when Mr. Wolf was about							
to freeze to death, he saw a small							
house in the woods. Smoke was							
coming from the chimney, so he							
knocked on the door. No one was							
home, but a note on the door said:							
Come in and make yourself warm.							
I'll be back about 2:00 p.m.							
Love,							
Granny							
The poor wet wolf came in and							
began to warm himself by // *the*							
fire.							
TOTALS							

Notes:

Examiner's Summary of Miscue Patterns:

PART III: DEVELOPMENTAL/PERFORMANCE SUMMARY

Silent Reading Comprehension

_____ 0–1 questions missed = Easy

_____ 2 questions missed = Adequate

_____ 3+ questions missed = Too hard

Oral Reading Accuracy

_____ 0–1 oral errors = Easy

_____ 2–5 oral errors = Adequate

_____ 6+ oral errors = Too hard

Continue to next assessment level passage? _____ Yes _____ No

Examiner's Notes:

The Terrible Lunch Contest (250 words)

PART I: SILENT READING COMPREHENSION

Background Statement: "This is a story about two students who didn't like the school lunchroom food. Read to find out what happened when they decided to see who could bring the most terrible lunch to school. Please read the story carefully because I'm going to ask you to tell me about it when you are through."

Teacher Directions: Once the student completes the silent reading, say, "Tell me about the story you just read." Check off any answers to the questions below that the student provides during the retelling. Ask all remaining questions not addressed during the retelling.

Questions/Answers	*Story Grammar Element/ Level of Comprehension*
_____1. Who were the two main people in the story? *(Jason and Chris)*	character-characterization/ literal
_____2. What was Jason's and Chris's problem? *(they didn't like the food in the lunchroom)*	story problem(s)/inferential
_____3. What did Jason and Chris decide to do about their problem? *(hold a terrible lunch contest)*	problem resolution attempts/ literal
_____4. Where did the contest take place? *(school lunchroom)*	setting/inferential
_____5. Why did Jason say Mrs. Smith had won the contest? *(neither could eat the sandwich he had made)*	problem resolution/ inferential
_____6. What happened after the contest? *(the boys didn't mind eating lunchroom food)*	problem resolution attempts/ literal
_____7. How would you describe Jason and Chris? *(funny, silly, or other plausible response)*	character-characterization/ evaluative
_____8. What would you say was the lesson learned by the boys? *(responses will vary but should indicate a theme/moral related to "things aren't as bad as they seem")*	theme/evaluative

PART II: ORAL READING AND ANALYSIS OF MISCUES

Directions: Say, "Now I would like to hear you read this story out loud." Have the student read orally until the 100-word sample is completed. Follow along on the Miscue Grid, marking any oral reading errors as appropriate. *Remember to count miscues only up to the point in the story containing the oral reading stop-marker (//).* Then complete the Developmental/Performance Summary to determine whether to continue the assessment. (*Note:* The Miscue Grid should be completed *after* the assessment session has been concluded in order to minimize stress for the student.)

	MIS-PRONUN.	SUB-STITUTION	OMISSION	INSERTION	TCHR. ASSIST.	SELF-CORRECT.	MEANING DISRUPTION
The Terrible Lunch Contest							
Jason and Chris didn't like the							
lunches at their school. They thought							
anything would taste better than							
the soybean hamburgers they had							
every Wednesday. They also							
didn't like the cardboard-tasting							
pizza on Fridays. One day							
Chris said, "Wouldn't it be							
funny if we had a terrible lunch							
contest? You know, we could							
see who could bring a lunch that is							
worse than the lunchroom food."							
Jason said, "OK,							
but the winner has to eat							
whatever he brings. The loser							
has to buy the winner a candy bar."							
The contest was on. The very next							
Wednesday the boys were ready. **//**							
TOTALS							

Notes:

Examiner's Summary of Miscue Patterns:

PART III: DEVELOPMENTAL/PERFORMANCE SUMMARY

Silent Reading Comprehension

_____ 0–1 questions missed = Easy

_____ 2   questions missed = Adequate

_____ 3+   questions missed = Too hard

Oral Reading Accuracy

_____ 0–1 oral errors = Easy

_____ 2–5 oral errors = Adequate

_____ 6+   oral errors = Too hard

Continue to next assessment level passage?   _____ Yes   _____ No

Examiner's Notes:

◢◣ FORM A: LEVEL 5 ASSESSMENT PROTOCOLS ◢◣

Hot Shoes (324 words)

PART I: SILENT READING COMPREHENSION

Background Statement: "This story is about how one group of boys feel about their athletic shoes. Read this story to find out how important special shoes are to playing sports. Read it carefully because I will ask you to tell me about it when you finish."

Teacher Directions: Once the student completes the silent reading, say, "Tell me about the story you just read." Check off any answers to the questions below that the student provides during the retelling. Ask all remaining questions not addressed during the retelling.

Questions/Answers	*Story Grammar Element/ Level of Comprehension*
_____ 1. Where did the story take place? *(I. B. Belcher Elementary School or at a school)*	setting/literal
_____ 2. Who were the two main characters in the story? *(Jamie Lee and Josh Kidder)*	character-characterization/ literal
_____ 3. What was the problem between Jamie and Josh? *(Jamie didn't think Josh could be a good player because of his shoes, Josh didn't fit in, or other plausible response)*	story problem(s)/inferential
_____ 4. How did Josh solve his problem with the other boys? *(he outplayed all of them)*	problem resolution/ inferential
_____ 5. What kind of person was Jamie Lee? *(conceited, stuck-up, or other plausible responses)*	character-characterization/ evaluative
_____ 6. What happened after the game? *(the other boys gathered around and asked Josh his secret)*	problem resolution attempts/ literal
_____ 7. Why did everyone laugh when Josh said, "Two things—lots of practice and cheap shoes"? *(because everything had happened because of his cheap shoes)*	problem resolution attempts/ inferential
_____ 8. What lesson does this story teach? *(responses will vary but should indicate a theme/moral related to "it's not what you wear that makes you good in a sport")*	theme/evaluative

PART II: ORAL READING AND ANALYSIS OF MISCUES

Directions: Say, "Now I would like to hear you read this story out loud." Have the student read orally until the 100-word sample is completed. Follow along on the Miscue Grid, marking any oral reading errors as appropriate. *Remember to count miscues only up to the point in the story containing the oral reading stop-marker (//).* Then complete the Developmental/Performance Summary to determine whether to continue the assessment. (*Note:* The Miscue Grid should be completed *after* the assessment session has been concluded in order to minimize stress for the student.)

	MIS-PRONUN.	SUB-STITUTION	OMISSION	INSERTION	TCHR. ASSIST.	SELF-CORRECT.	MEANING DISRUPTION
Hot Shoes							
The guys at the I. B. Belcher							
Elementary School loved all the							
new sport shoes. Some wore the							
"Sky High" model by Leader.							
Others who couldn't afford Sky							
Highs would settle for a lesser							
shoe. Some liked the "Street							
Smarts" by Master, or the							
"Uptown-Downtown" by Beebop.							
The Belcher boys got to the point							
with their shoes that they could							
identify their friends just by							
looking at their feet. But the boy							
who was the envy of the entire fifth							
grade was Jamie Lee. He had a							
pair of "High Five Pump 'em Ups"							
by Superior. The only thing Belcher							
boys // *loved as much as their*							
shoes was basketball.							
TOTALS							

Notes:

Examiner's Summary of Miscue Patterns:

PART III: DEVELOPMENTAL/PERFORMANCE SUMMARY

Silent Reading Comprehension

_____ 0–1 questions missed = Easy

_____ 2   questions missed = Adequate

_____ 3+   questions missed = Too hard

Oral Reading Accuracy

_____ 0–1 oral errors = Easy

_____ 2–5 oral errors = Adequate

_____ 6+   oral errors = Too hard

Continue to next assessment level passage? _____ Yes _____ No

Examiner's Notes:

Mountain Fire (367 words)

PART I: SILENT READING COMPREHENSION

Background Statement: "This story is about two boys who are lost on a mountain. Read the story to find out what they did to find their way home and what were the results of their problem resolution attempts. Read it carefully because I will ask you to tell me about what you read."

Teacher Directions: Once the student completes the silent reading, say, "Tell me about the story you just read." Check off any answers to the questions below that the student provides during the retelling. Ask all remaining questions not addressed during the retelling.

Questions/Answers	*Story Grammar Element/ Level of Comprehension*
_____1. Where did the story take place? *(Mount Holyoak)*	setting/literal
_____2. Who were the two boys in the story? *(Brad, Kevin)*	character-characterization/ literal
_____3. Why were the boys sent upstream by Brad's father? *(to look for cougar tracks)*	problem resolution attempts/ inferential
_____4. What was Brad's and Kevin's problem after going upstream? *(they became lost)*	story problem(s)/literal
_____5. What did the boys do to be found? *(they started a fire)*	problem resolution/ literal
_____6. What happened after their fire got out of hand? *(people came and put the fire out; other specifics related to this question are acceptable)*	problem resolution attempts/ literal
_____7. After the forest fire was put out, what did the boys do? *(helped reforest the area)*	problem resolution attempts/ literal
_____8. What new problem resulted from the forest fire? *(cougars were no longer in the area)*	story problem(s)/inferential

PART II: ORAL READING AND ANALYSIS OF MISCUES

Directions: Say, "Now I would like to hear you read this story out loud." Have the student read orally until the 100-word sample is completed. Follow along on the Miscue Grid, marking any oral reading errors as appropriate. *Remember to count miscues only up to the point in the story containing the oral reading stop-marker (//).* Then complete the Developmental/Performance Summary to determine whether to continue the assessment. (*Note:* The Miscue Grid should be completed *after* the assessment session has been concluded in order to minimize stress for the student.)

	MIS-PRONUN.	SUB-STITUTION	OMISSION	INSERTION	TCHR. ASSIST.	SELF-CORRECT.	MEANING DISRUPTION
Mountain Fire							
One August afternoon Brad and							
Kevin went tracking with their							
fathers on Mount Holyoak. Brad's							
father was a conservationist for the							
Forest Service and was searching							
for evidence of cougars. Many people							
feared that the cougars were extinct on							
Mount Holyoak. The boys became							
excited when they found what appeared							
to be a partial cougar track near							
a stream. But as the day wore on, no							
new tracks were found. After lunch							
Brad's father sent the boys upstream							
while he circled west. He told the							
boys to return to the lunch site							
in an hour. After about forty-five							
minutes, // *the boys found the stream's*							
source and could follow it no							
more.							
TOTALS							

Notes:

Examiner's Summary of Miscue Patterns:

PART III: DEVELOPMENTAL/PERFORMANCE SUMMARY

Silent Reading Comprehension

_____ 0–1 questions missed = Easy

_____ 2 questions missed = Adequate

_____ 3+ questions missed = Too hard

Oral Reading Accuracy

_____ 0–1 oral errors = Easy

_____ 2–5 oral errors = Adequate

_____ 6+ oral errors = Too hard

Continue to next assessment level passage? _____ Yes _____ No

Examiner's Notes:

FORM A: LEVEL 7 ASSESSMENT PROTOCOLS

The Canoe Trip (490 words)

PART I: SILENT READING COMPREHENSION

Background Statement: "This story is about two girls who take a canoe trip. Read the story and find out what happens to the girls while canoeing. Read it carefully because I'm going to ask you to tell me about it when you finish."

Teacher Directions: Once the student completes the silent reading, say, "Tell me about the story you just read." Check off any answers to the questions below that the student provides during the retelling. Ask all remaining questions not addressed during the retelling.

Questions/Answers	*Story Grammar Element/ Level of Comprehension*
_____1. Where did this story take place? (*West Yellowstone*)	setting/literal
_____2. Who was the story mainly about? (*Katherine and Amy*)	character-characterization/ literal
_____3. What was the girls' problem? (*they capsized their canoe*)	story problem(s)/literal
_____4. What happened after they capsized? (*they lost their food but saved the canoe*)	problem resolution attempts/ inferential
_____5. Why couldn't the girls catch up with the floating coolers? (*because of the time it took to empty the canoe and the swiftness of the water*)	problem resolution attempts/ inferential
_____6. How did the problem of the lost food turn out? (*Katherine's parents caught the floating coolers*)	story solution/literal
_____7. How did Katherine and Amy feel after reaching Katherine's parents? (*relieved, embarrassed, or other plausible response*)	character-characterization/ evaluative
_____8. Why is "all's well that ends well" a good theme for this story? (*responses will vary but should reflect the fact that the girls didn't give up and everything turned out fine when they reached Katherine's parents*)	theme/evaluative

PART II: ORAL READING AND ANALYSIS OF MISCUES

Directions: Say, "Now I would like to hear you read this story out loud." Have the student read orally until the 100-word sample is completed. Follow along on the Miscue Grid, marking any oral reading errors as appropriate. *Remember to count miscues only up to the point in the story containing the oral reading stop-marker (//).* Then complete the Developmental/Performance Summary to determine whether to continue the assessment. (*Note:* The Miscue Grid should be completed *after* the assessment session has been concluded in order to minimize stress for the student.)

	MIS-PRONUN.	SUB-STITUTION	OMISSION	INSERTION	TCHR. ASSIST.	SELF-CORRECT.	MEANING DISRUPTION
The Canoe Trip							
Katherine and her family like to							
spend their vacation camping out.							
Frequently they go to either							
Great Smoky Mountains National							
Park or Yellowstone National Park.							
Since they have camped out							
for many years, they have become							
quite accomplished. Katherine is able							
to start a fire with flint and steel,							
build a lean-to for shelter, and							
find food in the forest on							
which to live. Katherine's favorite							
outdoor activity is canoeing. Although							
she is quite a good canoer, there is							
one canoe trip that she'll never forget.							
It was a canoe trip she took with							
her family and her friend // *Amy*							
down the Madison River near							
West Yellowstone.							
TOTALS							

Notes:

Examiner's Summary of Miscue Patterns:

PART III: DEVELOPMENTAL/PERFORMANCE SUMMARY

Silent Reading Comprehension

_____ 0–1 questions missed = Easy

_____ 2 questions missed = Adequate

_____ 3+ questions missed = Too hard

Oral Reading Accuracy

_____ 0–1 oral errors = Easy

_____ 2–5 oral errors = Adequate

_____ 6+ oral errors = Too hard

Continue to next assessment level passage? _____ Yes _____ No

Examiner's Notes:

The Eagle (504 words)

PART I: SILENT READING COMPREHENSION

Background Statement: "This story is an old Native American tale about an eagle. Read the passage and try to identify the message the story tells. Read it carefully because I'm going to ask you to tell me about it when you finish."

Teacher Directions: Once the student completes the silent reading, say, "Tell me about the story you just read." Check off any answers to the questions below that the student provides during the retelling. Ask all remaining questions not addressed during the retelling.

Questions/Answers	*Story Grammar Element/ Level of Comprehension*
_____1. Where does the story take place? *(mountain and farm)*	setting/literal
_____2. Who were the people in the story? *(Hopi farmer, his son, and Anasazi brave)*	character-characterization/ literal
_____3. What was the problem presented in the story? *(convincing the eagle that he wasn't a chicken)*	story problem(s)/inferential
_____4. What did the eagle do that was like a chicken? *(scratching, pecking at food, wouldn't fly)*	problem resolution attempts/ literal
_____5. What was the brave's first attempt to convince the bird it was an eagle? *(tried to get it to fly from barn)*	problem resolution attempts/ literal
_____6. How did the brave finally get the bird to recognize it could fly? *(by taking it up to a high bluff so that it could see the valley and sense freedom)*	problem resolution/ literal
_____7. What words would you use to describe the farmer? *(responses will vary but should relate to the farmer being deceitful, uncaring, or a liar)*	character-characterization/ evaluative
_____8. What lesson does this story teach? *(responses will vary but should indicate a theme/ moral related to "you are what you think you are")*	theme/evaluative

PART II: ORAL READING AND ANALYSIS OF MISCUES

Directions: Say, "Now I would like to hear you read this story out loud." Have the student read orally until the 100-word sample is completed. Follow along on the Miscue Grid, marking any oral reading errors as appropriate. *Remember to count miscues only up to the point in the story containing the oral reading stop-marker (//).* Then complete the Developmental/Performance Summary to determine whether to continue the assessment. (*Note:* The Miscue Grid should be completed *after* the assessment session has been concluded in order to minimize stress for the student.)

	MIS-PRONUN.	SUB-STITUTION	OMISSION	INSERTION	TCHR. ASSIST.	SELF-CORRECT.	MEANING DISRUPTION
The Eagle							
There exists an old Native American							
legend about an eagle who thought							
he was a chicken. It seems that							
a Hopi farmer and his only son							
decided to climb a nearby mountain							
to observe an eagle's nest.							
The trip would take them all							
day, so they brought along some							
rations and water for the trek.							
The man and the boy crossed the							
enormous fields of maize and beans							
into the foothills. Soon thereafter							
they were ascending the mountain							
and the climb became rigorous							
and hazardous. They occasionally							
looked back toward their home and							
at the panoramic view of the entire //							
valley. Finally the farmer and son							
reached the mountain's summit.							
TOTALS							

Notes:

Examiner's Summary of Miscue Patterns:

PART III: DEVELOPMENTAL/PERFORMANCE SUMMARY

Silent Reading Comprehension

_____ 0–1 questions missed = Easy

_____ 2 questions missed = Adequate

_____ 3+ questions missed = Too hard

Oral Reading Accuracy

_____ 0–1 oral errors = Easy

_____ 2–5 oral errors = Adequate

_____ 6+ oral errors = Too hard

Continue to next assessment level passage? _____ Yes _____ No

Examiner's Notes:

The Case of Angela Violet (378 words)

PART I: SILENT READING COMPREHENSION

Background Statement: "This story is about a young girl's disappearance. Read the story carefully because I will ask you to tell it to me when you finish."

Teacher Directions: Once the student completes the silent reading, say, "Tell me about the story you just read." Check off any answers to the questions below that the student provides during the retelling. Ask all remaining questions not addressed during the retelling.

Questions/Answers   *Story Grammar Element/*
                                                        Level of Comprehension

_____1. What time of year did the story take place?   setting/literal
        (autumn)

_____2. What was the main problem in the story?   story problem(s)/inferential
        (Katrina Bowers had disappeared)

_____3. What problem resolution attempts did the   problem resolution attempts/
        authorities take when they received the   literal
        telephone tip?
        *(got a search warrant and went to Miss Violet's
        house)*

_____4. How was Katrina's case finally solved?   problem resolution/literal
        (she was found in California)

_____5. What was Miss Violet's reaction   problem resolution attempts/
        to the police wanting to search her house?   literal
        (she didn't mind, she welcomed the search)

_____6. What kind of person was Miss Violet?   character-characterization/
        *(responses will vary but should suggest   inferential
        kind, caring, gentle, lonely)*

_____7. What did the people in the community   problem resolution attempts/
        do after Miss Violet was proved innocent?   literal
        (began to do things for and with her)

_____8. What is the lesson of this story?   theme/evaluative
        *(responses will vary but should indicate
        a theme/moral related to "you can't judge a
        book by its cover")*

PART II: ORAL READING AND ANALYSIS OF MISCUES

Directions: Say, "Now I would like to hear you read this story out loud." Have the student read orally until the 100-word sample is completed. Follow along on the Miscue Grid, marking any oral reading errors as appropriate. *Remember to count miscues only up to the point in the story containing the oral reading stop-marker (//).* Then complete the Developmental/Performance Summary to determine whether to continue the assessment. (*Note:* The Miscue Grid should be completed *after* the assessment session has been concluded in order to minimize stress for the student.)

	MIS-PRONUN.	SUB-STITUTION	OMISSION	INSERTION	TCHR. ASSIST.	SELF-CORRECT.	MEANING DISRUPTION
The Case of Angela Violet							
Angela Violet was an elderly lady in							
our neighborhood who some people							
thought suspicious. She was rarely seen							
outside her spacious Victorian-styled							
home, and then only to retrieve the daily							
mail. Her pasty complexion and ancient							
dress made her appear like an apparition.							
Small children in the neighborhood							
speculated that she might be some							
sort of witch. It appeared that Miss							
Violet had no contact with the outside							
world. One autumn day news spread							
through the community that a high							
school cheerleader, Katrina Bowers,							
had disappeared. It was feared by the							
police that Katrina had been abducted.							
State and // *local police joined forces*							
with the Federal Bureau of Investigation							
in the massive search effort.							
TOTALS							

Notes:

Examiner's Summary of Miscue Patterns:

PART III: DEVELOPMENTAL/PERFORMANCE SUMMARY

Silent Reading Comprehension   *Oral Reading Accuracy*

_____ 0–1 questions missed = Easy   _____ 0–1 oral errors = Easy

_____ 2   questions missed = Adequate   _____ 2–5 oral errors = Adequate

_____ 3+   questions missed = Too hard   _____ 6+   oral errors = Too hard

Continue to next assessment level passage?   _____ Yes   _____ No

Examiner's Notes:

Form B
Sentences for Initial
Passage Selection

FORM B: LEVEL 1

1. Today is my birthday.

2. I wanted to have a party.

3. She stopped at the trees.

FORM B: LEVEL 2

1. We have extra leaves to rake.

2. I need some extra money.

3. She heard me in the kitchen.

FORM B: LEVEL 3

1. I was beginning to get afraid.

2. He could hear the voice get closer.

3. Tomorrow I will finish my work.

FORM B: LEVEL 4

1. She walked carefully into the darkness.

2. I know it is important to eat vegetables.

3. He slipped as he reached up into the oak tree.

FORM B: LEVEL 5

1. The tree withered away after the storm.

2. The neighborhood was shaken after the fire.

3. I was frightened by my dream.

FORM B: LEVEL 6

1. By not participating, he was barely passing in school.

2. I allowed the gifted students extra time.

3. Especially high achievement is a result of good instruction.

FORM B: LEVEL 7

1. I made an appointment to purchase the bike.

2. The plastic covering the application form was especially thick.

3. His robust legs made a difference in his overall physical strength.

FORM B: LEVEL 8

1. He was provoked because he was small in stature.

2. The familiar mockery led to the fight.

3. His bruised ego never really recovered.

FORM B: LEVEL 9

1. Her nontraditional dress improved her appearance.

2. The anonymous letter wasn't taken seriously.

3. He was a formidable-looking person, even wearing a sleazy coat.

FORM B
Narrative Passages

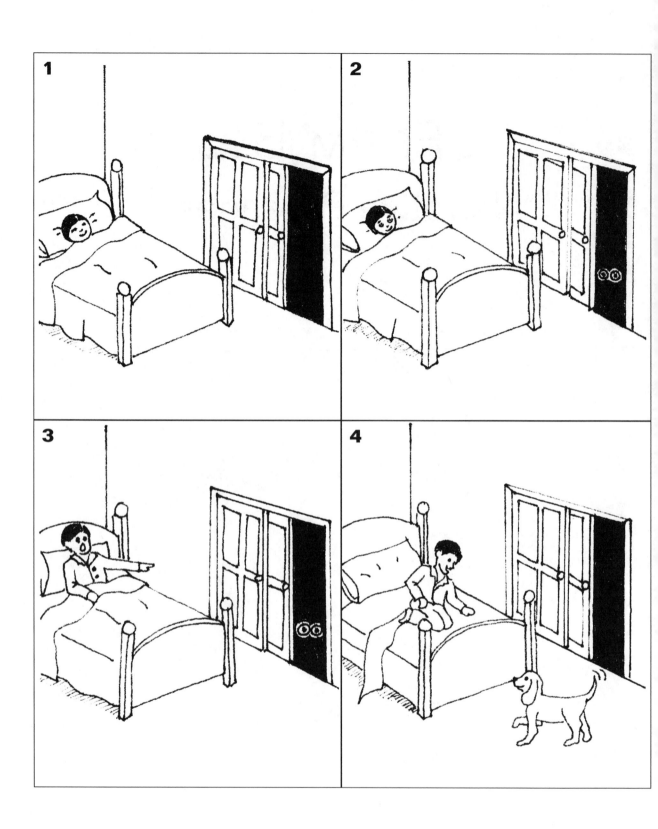

1 I like to play T-ball at school.

2 On Friday we played the big game.

3 I got a hit at the end of the game.

4 I made it home and won the game.

Birthday at the Zoo

It was Sunday.

I got out of bed and went to eat.

Mom said, "Today is your birthday, Pat. What do you want to do?"

I wanted a party but I did not tell Mom.

I said, "I just want to play."

Mom said, "Come take a ride with me."

I got in the car and soon we were in the city.

The car stopped. We got out.

We walked past some trees and I saw a sign that said "City Zoo."

All my friends were at the gate.

I was all smiles. Mom had planned a party for me.

It was the best birthday ever.

Mary's New Bike

Mary wanted a new bike. She helped around the house to make money. She had even helped her Father rake leaves for extra money. But she still didn't have the money for the new ten-speed bike.

One day her Aunt Deb came to visit Mary's family. Aunt Deb heard that Mary wanted a new bike. She told Mary that she had some work for her. Mary walked over to Aunt Deb's house the very next day.

Aunt Deb had Mary mop her kitchen floor. Mary cleaned out the flower beds. Mary swept out the carport. Finally Aunt Deb asked Mary to fold her clean clothes. Mary was tired by the end of the day. But when Aunt Deb paid Mary her money, Mary smiled and hugged Aunt Deb. She hurried home to tell her parents the good news. They smiled and told her how proud they were.

The next day Mary went to the store.

Bedtime

The sun was going down. The air was hot and Wild Willie was afraid. Never had he been in such a dry, hot place. His horse, Wizard, was trying to find a few blades of grass. Wild Willie was beginning to fall asleep from staying awake so long. Then he heard the sound again—the same sound he had been hearing for days. What could it be? Why was it following him? How could he find out what or who it was?

Slowly Wizard turned around. Willie stood up in the stirrups to see over the sand dune. He saw no one. Again he heard the sound. This time it came from behind. It was a slow rumbling sound. He got off his horse. He took his gun and got ready. Slowly the sound came closer and closer. Willie raised his gun. . . .

Then the TV went off and a voice said, "Beth, it's time to go to bed. Tomorrow is a school day and it's getting late." "Aw, Mom, can't I finish seeing the show?" I asked. "No, you can watch it another time," my mother replied.

As I went slowly upstairs to bed, I wondered what Wild Willie had seen. Maybe it had been some kind of animal or just a person in a wagon. But it was probably the Ghost of the Sand Wind. Yeah, that had to be it. Other people had claimed to have seen it. But I won't know until the reruns.

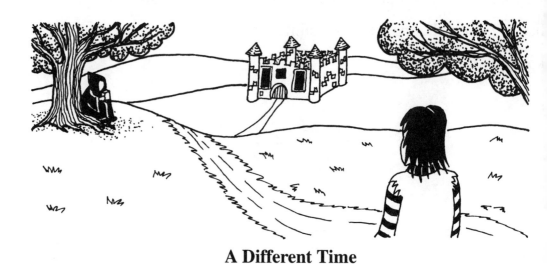

A Different Time

Marlo lived in a different time and a different place. He lived in a time of darkness and gloom. Marlo lived in a small hut with his poor parents. He didn't have nice clothes and he didn't have much to eat. But neither of these things bothered Marlo. There was only one thing he wanted. But he couldn't have it because the ruler would not let any of his people have it. This most important thing was to be able to read. Today this may seem like a dumb wish, but to Marlo it wasn't.

One day Marlo's father sent him to the castle with a cart of vegetables. On the way Marlo met an old man who had strange eyes. The old man's head was hooded, but his eyes were deep blue and sparkled. The old man asked Marlo if he could please have a few vegetables to eat. Marlo agreed even though he knew he would get into trouble. When the old man finished, he said, "Come to the old oak tree tonight and the future will be yours." Marlo walked away wondering what the old man meant.

That night Marlo slipped out of the hut. He ran up the road until he reached the old oak tree. There he found the old man sitting on the ground.

The old man stood up and handed Marlo a box. He said, "Marlo, inside this box is what you want. Your life will never be the same."

Marlo took the box, looked down for a second, and then the old man was nowhere to be seen. Marlo rushed home. He carefully opened the box. And there in the light of his one candle Marlo saw what was in the box. It was a book.

Afternoon Walk

One day Allison was walking in the woods behind her house. Some of the other children in the neighborhood liked to tease her by saying that the woods were haunted. "There's an old, withered, witch-like woman in those woods who comes out at two o'clock every day to catch children," they'd say. "She makes them do housework and things like that. Then she sells them to a grim looking dwarf from far away when they are too tired to work. Once captured they are never seen again." Allison knew her friends were only telling stories, but it still frightened her sometimes when she went into the woods.

On this particular morning, Allison thought she would take a short stroll to find wild flowers for her Mother. After walking for an hour or so, she stopped to rest under an elm tree. Unfortunately she fell fast asleep. The next thing she knew, Allison was being shaken by a terribly ugly old woman dressed all in black. Startled, Allison looked at her watch. It was two o'clock. The old woman took Allison to a run-down old hut.

For what seemed like hours, Allison had to wash dishes, clean out a doghouse, and scrub floors. While cleaning out the doghouse, she found a dog tag that read "Spirit." She tucked it into her pocket thinking she would give it to the woman later. The old woman checked on Allison every few minutes. She always asked Allison if she were tired. Allison always said that she wasn't tired because she remembered the story of the dwarf.

It was just after Allison finished the doghouse that her chance to escape occurred. The old woman went into a back room calling for Spirit so Allison quickly ran out the door. Allison ran and ran until she finally couldn't run any farther. She lay down under an elm tree and fell asleep.

Allison was awakened by her brother who said, "Mom says it's getting late and you'd better come home quick." Allison said, "Oh, boy, what an awful dream I just had." She told her brother all about her dream on the way home. All he said was, "Get serious."

That night when Allison undressed to take her bath, a small metal tag fell from her pocket that had "Spirit" printed on it.

Laser Boy

My name is Bob and I'm a teacher. Several years ago I knew a student that I'd like to tell you about.

Matthew was a 13-year-old who never seemed to do well in school. Some say that he was a misfit, someone who doesn't quite fit in with the other kids his age. Not only that, Matthew had trouble in school nearly his whole life. He failed to complete his homework even when it was an easy assignment. By not participating in class, not turning in homework, and only doing a fair job on tests, Matthew always seemed to be just barely passing.

One day when Matthew was in seventh grade his teacher decided to find out what Matthew's problem was in school. The teacher had him tested and found out from the special education teacher that Matthew was gifted in the areas of science and mathematics! The special education teacher said, "Oh, yes, sometimes students who do poorly in school are quite gifted. They just haven't been allowed to show what they can do. Also, some gifted students are not especially strong in some school subjects. But they are excellent in music, working with mechanical objects, or even athletics."

After Matthew's discovery was made, he was asked what he was interested in studying. Matthew answered that he wanted to study lasers. For the rest of that year, Matthew read everything he could find in the library at the university having to do with lasers. Later, a professor in California was found who was an expert on laser technology. The professor agreed to talk with Matthew on a regular basis to help answer questions or solve any problems Matthew had.

During the last part of seventh grade, Matthew worked on a special science project. He built a model laser. It was fantastic! Matthew's model was accurate to the last detail. Everyone was very impressed with his project. All the kids at school began calling him "laser boy." He found new friends and his life at school and home greatly improved.

Since that very special year when I got to know "laser boy," I've looked at students who are experiencing trouble in a new way. I'm convinced that everyone has special talents. We only need to discover what they are.

The Paper Route

Scott had a chance to earn his own money for the first time. Answering an advertisement for newspaper carriers, he set up an appointment with Mr. Miley, the distribution manager. Mr. Miley was a rather short and stocky man who spoke with a loud voice.

After reviewing Scott's application, Mr. Miley said, "You look like a dependable young man to me. Do your parents approve of your becoming a paperboy?" "Yes, sir," replied Scott, "and I have a letter from my Dad saying it's OK with him."

"You can have the job, Scott," said Mr. Miley. "However, I want you to realize that this is a long route and you will have to get up very early. You will also have to have robust legs and a good bike," warned Mr. Miley.

Getting started was not easy. Scott had to be out of bed by 4:30 A.M. Next he had to pick up the papers and roll them up for placement in a plastic bag. He would usually finish that much by 5:30 A.M. Then it was time to deliver the papers.

Most days Scott could deliver all his newspapers in just two trips. His father had purchased a new bike for Scott and attached an enormous basket to it. The really hard days were Thursday and Sunday. Newspapers were especially large on those days. Scott would have to make as many as five trips to get the papers delivered on those days.

The good part of the job was, of course, the money. Scott found that he was making about 250 dollars a month. He was also developing his physical strength. But the negative side of the job was bad weather and cranky customers. When it rained, Scott got drenched. When it snowed, Scott froze. Scott's biggest complaint was his cranky customers, particularly Mr. Gripper. Mr. Gripper insisted on his paper being put in his mailbox, rain or shine. If Scott failed to do this, Mr. Gripper always called the newspaper office and complained. But Scott avoided most complaints by going out of his way to please his customers.

After one year on the job, Scott was called into Mr. Miley's office for an end-of-year conference. During the year Scott had managed to save 1,300 dollars and pay back his father for the bike. So when Mr. Miley asked him if he wanted to continue working for the paper, Scott said, "Yes." But he added, "It was a lot more work than I counted on and I could live without the Mr. Grippers of the world. But I really like the work."

Riley and Leonard

At times Leonard felt like the most unpopular boy in school. No matter what he did he was constantly ridiculed by his classmates. Maybe it was because he was small in stature and wore thick bifocals. Or maybe it was because he didn't like sports. Possibly it was because he couldn't afford the designer clothes the other kids seemed to live for. Regardless, Leonard felt like a loser and was unhappy with his situation.

One day, while putting his books in his locker, the familiar mockery began. A small covey of classmates formed a semicircle around Leonard. Each began to taunt him and call him names. Most joined in after Riley McClure made Leonard drop his books. They all laughed and called him *bozo*, *nerd*, and *dweeb*. But Leonard tried not to be provoked; that is, until Riley made horrible slurs about Leonard's family and particularly Leonard's mother. Leonard couldn't resist. He lunged at Riley but Riley was much bigger and Leonard's attack ended in disaster. Riley slammed him into the lockers, grabbed Leonard by the throat, and made Leonard holler "calf rope," a sign of total submission.

As the group disbanded, so they wouldn't be late for their next class, Lorrie Warner approached Leonard. She apologized for the group's behavior and tried to comfort Leonard's hurt pride. She said, "What goes around, comes around." But her consoling didn't help Leonard's bruised ego.

Twenty years later Leonard found himself president of the largest bank in town. He was well respected in the community and was quite generous when it came to civic projects. Although he had never married, he had recently begun dating Lorrie Warner, his old classmate.

One Friday evening Leonard and Lorrie were eating at a fancy restaurant. They had finished their meal and were heading out the door when a beggar approached. The beggar requested money to buy food. There was something curious about the beggar that Leonard could not place. But being generous, Leonard gave the man ten dollars. The beggar was so surprised by the large amount that he shook Leonard's hand vigorously before quickly backing away into the street. Lorrie screamed a word of caution but it was too late. The beggar had stepped into the path of a truck and was struck broadside. Leonard and Lorrie waited for the ambulance to carry the man away.

The next morning the headlines carried the story of the beggar. He had died from internal injuries early that morning. As Leonard read the details, he suddenly dropped the paper and turned pale. The beggar's name was Riley McClure.

The Long Night

I arrived late at the New Orleans International Airport because of delays in St. Louis. The night was descending on the Crescent City as I entered the cab for the short ride to city center. As the cab headed toward the city, the cabbie engaged me in an informative conversation about the Crescent City. She had an island accent and her multicolored dress was very nontraditional. After I told her I wanted to go to Rampart in the French Quarter, she abruptly turned left and headed southwest.

Fifteen minutes later, without a word, I got out of the cab and proceeded up Rampart. I had gone only two blocks when I noticed that a bleak little man was following me. I say bleak because when I saw his silhouette under a fluorescent street light, he looked as if something mean and cruel had happened in his early life. You know, a kind of woebegone appearance. Every time I stopped, he stopped. If I sped up my pace, his pace quickened. Finally I slipped into an anonymous doorway. As he approached I swiftly reached out and grabbed him by his grimy coat. I asked him why he was following me but all he did was whimper and hand me a crumpled-up note. As my eyes fell on the note, he slipped out of my grasp and ran into the eerily approaching fog.

The note contained the following message: "Your death is behind you. Run if you value your life." I didn't think, I ran.

As I rounded the corner of Rampart and Royal, I ran straight into a policeman. I felt relief. I told him my story. He chuckled and didn't take me seriously. As he walked away I saw a set of eyes from behind a refuse container in an alleyway. I ran again.

As I cut through an alley I was accosted by two men with strange accents. They said they had been sent by Nero. They asked me where I had put the package. I told them I had no idea of what they were referring to. They gathered me up and forced me into a dingy building.

As soon as my eyes adjusted to the glow of the incandescent lights, I saw a large, rotund man at a table. He looked formidable. I was forced to sit across the table from the man. He leaned forward and I could see his face. A face of evil. He studied me carefully, and then he looked at my assailants. "This isn't Mouser, you idiots. Get him out of here." They blindfolded me and walked me out of the building a different way. An hour later I found myself on a deserted street.

Two days later I left the Crescent City. I never told anyone about my experience, and I've never been back.

FORM B

Examiner's Assessment Protocols

■ FORM B: PREPRIMER (PP) LEVEL ASSESSMENT PROTOCOL ■

Eyes in My Closet (Wordless picture story)

PART I: WORDLESS PICTURE STORY READING

Background Statement: "These pictures tell a story about a child who is going to bed. Look at each picture as I show it to you and think about the story the pictures tell. Later, I will want you to tell me the story using the pictures."

Teacher Directions: Refer the student to each picture slowly and in order as numbered. Do not comment on the pictures. Then repeat the procedure, asking the student to tell the story in the student's own words. Record the student's reading using a tape recorder, and transcribe the reading as it is being dictated. Replay the recording later to make sure that your transcription is accurate and complete.

PART II: EMERGENT READING BEHAVIOR CHECKLIST

Directions: Following are emergent reading behaviors identified through research and grouped according to broad developmental stages. Check all behaviors you have observed. *If the student progresses to Stage 3 or 4, continue your assessment using the Primer Level (P) passage.*

Stage 1: Early Connections to Reading—Describing Pictures

_____ Attends to and describes (labels) pictures in books

_____ Has a limited sense of story

_____ Follows verbal directions for this activity

_____ Uses oral vocabulary appropriate for age/grade level

_____ Displays attention span appropriate for age/grade level

_____ Responds to questions in an appropriate manner

_____ Appears to connect pictures (sees as being interrelated)

Stage 2: Connecting Pictures to Form Story

_____ Attends to pictures and develops oral stories across the pages of the book

_____ Uses only childlike or descriptive (storyteller) language to tell the story, rather than book language (i.e., Once upon a time...; There once was a little boy...)

Stage 3: Transitional Picture Reading

_____ Attends to pictures as a connected story

_____ Mixes storyteller language with book language

Stage 4: Advanced Picture Reading

_____ Attends to pictures and develops oral stories across the pages of the book

_____ Speaks as though reading the story (uses book language)

Examiner's Notes:

FORM B: PRIMER (P) LEVEL ASSESSMENT PROTOCOLS

The T-Ball Game (32 words)

PART I: PICTURE STORY READING—ORAL READING AND ANALYSIS OF MISCUES

Background Statement: "This is a story about a child who is playing a game. Let's look at each picture first. Now, read the story to yourself. Later, I will want you to read the story to me."

Teacher Directions: Refer the student to each frame of the story slowly and in order as numbered. Do not read the story or comment on the pictures. After the student has read the story silently, ask the student to read the story aloud. Record the student's reading using a tape recorder, and mark any miscues on the Miscue Grid provided. Following the oral reading, complete the Emergent Reading Behavior Checklist. Assessment information obtained from both the Miscue Grid and the Emergent Reading Behavior Checklist will help you to determine whether to continue your assessment. If the student is unable to read the passage independently the first time, read it aloud, then ask the student to try to read the story again. This will help you to understand whether the student is able to memorize and repeat text, an important developmental milestone (see the *Instructions for Administering the Preprimer (PP) and Primer (P) Passages* section in the front of this book for more information). The assessment should stop after this activity, if the child is unable to read the text independently. (Note: The Miscue Grid should be completed *after* the assessment session has been concluded in order to minimize stress for the student.)

	MIS-PRONUN.	SUB-STITUTION	OMISSION	INSERTION	TCHR. ASSIST.	SELF-CORRECT.	MEANING DISRUPTION
The T-Ball Game							
I like to play T-ball							
at school. On Friday							
we played the big							
game. I got a							
hit at the end of							
the game. I made							
it home and won							
the game.							
TOTALS							

Notes:

PART II: EMERGENT READING BEHAVIOR CHECKLIST

Directions: Following are emergent reading behaviors identified through research and grouped according to broad developmental stages. After completing the oral reading, check each behavior observed below to help determine development level and whether to continue the assessment. *If the student seems to be at Stage 6 or 7 and the oral reading scored at an Easy or Adequate level, continue the assessment using the Level 1 passage.*

Stage 5: Early Print Reading

_____ Tells a story using the pictures

_____ Knows print moves from left to right, top to bottom

_____ Creates part of the text using book language and knows some words on sight

Stage 6: Early Strategic Reading

_____ Uses context to guess at some unknown words (guesses make sense)

_____ Notices beginning sounds in words and uses them in guessing unknown words

_____ Seems to sometimes use syntax to help identify words in print

_____ Recognizes some word parts, such as root words and affixes

Stage 7: Moderate Strategic Reading

_____ Sometimes uses context and word parts to decode words

_____ Self-corrects when making an oral reading miscue

_____ Retells the passage easily and may embellish the storyline

_____ Shows some awareness of vowel sounds

Examiner's Notes

Examiner's Summary of Miscue Patterns:

PART III: DEVELOPMENTAL/PERFORMANCE SUMMARY

Silent Reading Comprehension

_____ 0–1 questions missed = Easy

_____ 2 questions missed = Adequate

_____ 3+ questions missed = Too hard

Oral Reading Accuracy

_____ 0–1 oral errors = Easy

_____ 2–5 oral errors = Adequate

_____ 6+ oral errors = Too hard

Continue to next assessment level passage? _____ Yes _____ No

Examiner's Notes:

FORM B: LEVEL 1 ASSESSMENT PROTOCOLS

Birthday at the Zoo (106 words)

PART I: SILENT READING COMPREHENSION

Background Statement: "What do you like to do on your birthday? Read this story carefully to find out what special thing a girl wanted for her birthday. I'm going to ask you to tell me about the story when you're through reading it."

Teacher Directions: Once the student completes the silent reading, say, "Tell me about the story you just read." Check off any answers to the questions below that the student provides during the retelling. Ask all remaining questions not addressed during the retelling.

Questions/Answers	*Story Grammar Element/ Level of Comprehension*
_____1. Who were the people in the story? *(Pat and her Mom)*	character-characterization/ literal
_____2. What was Pat's wish? *(Pat wanted to have a party)*	story problem(s)/literal
_____3. What did Pat say she wanted to do for her birthday? *(just play)*	problem resolution attempts/ literal
_____4. Did Pat get her wish? How do you know? *(yes, she had a surprise party at the zoo)*	problem resolution/ literal
_____5. How did Pat and her Mom get to the zoo? *(drove in by car)*	problem resolution attempts/ literal
_____6. What words would you use to describe how Pat felt at the zoo? *(surprised, happy, etc.)*	character-characterization/ inferential
_____7. Where was Pat when the story began? *(in her bedroom or house)*	setting/inferential
_____8. When did Pat first know that she was going to have a birthday party? *(when she got to the zoo and saw her friends)*	problem resolution attempts/ inferential

PART II: ORAL READING AND ANALYSIS OF MISCUES

Directions: Say, "Now I would like to hear you read this story out loud." Have the student read orally until the 100-word sample is completed. Follow along on the Miscue Grid, marking any oral reading errors as appropriate. *Remember to count miscues only up to the point in the story containing the oral reading stop-marker (//).* Then complete the Developmental/Performance Summary to determine whether to continue the assessment. (*Note:* The Miscue Grid should be completed *after* the assessment session has been concluded in order to minimize stress for the student.)

	MIS-PRONUN.	SUB-STITUTION	OMISSION	INSERTION	TCHR. ASSIST.	SELF-CORRECT.	MEANING DISRUPTION
Birthday at the Zoo							
It was Sunday.							
I got out of bed and went							
to eat. Mom said, "Today							
is your birthday, Pat. What							
do you want to do?" I wanted							
a party but I did not tell Mom.							
I said, "I just want to play."							
Mom said, "Come take							
a ride with me." I got							
in the car and soon we							
were in the city.							
The car stopped. We got							
out. We walked past some							
trees and I saw a sign that							
said "City Zoo." All my friends							
were at the gate. I was all smiles.							
Mom had planned a party for me. //							
It was the best birthday ever.							
TOTALS							

Notes:

Examiner's Summary of Miscue Patterns:

PART III: DEVELOPMENTAL/PERFORMANCE SUMMARY

Silent Reading Comprehension

_____ 0–1 questions missed = Easy

_____ 2   questions missed = Adequate

_____ 3+   questions missed = Too hard

Oral Reading Accuracy

_____ 0–1 oral errors = Easy

_____ 2–5 oral errors = Adequate

_____ 6+   oral errors = Too hard

Continue to next assessment level passage?   _____ Yes   _____ No

Examiner's Notes:

Mary's New Bike (156 words)

PART I: SILENT READING COMPREHENSION

Background Statement: "Have you ever tried to earn money for something special? Read this story to find out how Mary was able to earn something special. Read it carefully because I am going to ask you to tell me about the story when you finish."

Teacher Directions: Once the student completes the silent reading, say, "Tell me about the story you just read." Check off any answers to the questions below that the student provides during the retelling. Ask all remaining questions not addressed during the retelling.

Questions/Answers	*Story Grammar Element/ Level of Comprehension*
_____1. Who was this story about? *(Mary)*	character-characterization/ literal
_____2. What was Mary's problem in the story? *(she wanted a new bike but she didn't have enough money)*	story problem(s)/literal
_____3. What had Mary done to earn money in the past? *(rake leaves and help around the house)*	problem resolution attempts/ literal
_____4. Besides Mary, who were the people in the story? *(Aunt Deb, Mary's family)*	character-characterization/ literal
_____5. How did Mary finally solve her problem? *(worked hard for Aunt Deb and earned enough money)*	problem resolution/ inferential
_____6. What were two things Mary did for Aunt Deb? *(mopped floor, swept carport, cleaned out flower beds)*	problem resolution attempts/ literal
_____7. What lesson did Mary learn about getting something you really want? *(it takes time and hard work)*	theme/evaluative
_____8. Why did Mary go to the store the next day? *(to buy her bike)*	problem resolution attempts/ inferential

PART II: ORAL READING AND ANALYSIS OF MISCUES

Directions: Say, "Now I would like to hear you read this story out loud." Have the student read orally until the 100-word sample is completed. Follow along on the Miscue Grid, marking any oral reading errors as appropriate. *Remember to count miscues only up to the point in the story containing the oral reading stop-marker (//).* Then complete the Developmental/Performance Summary to determine whether to continue the assessment. (*Note:* The Miscue Grid should be completed *after* the assessment session has been concluded in order to minimize stress for the student.)

	MIS-PRONUN.	SUB-STITUTION	OMISSION	INSERTION	TCHR. ASSIST.	SELF-CORRECT.	MEANING DISRUPTION
Mary's New Bike							
Mary wanted a new bike. She							
helped around the house to make							
money. She had even helped her							
Father rake leaves for extra money.							
But she still didn't have the							
money for the new ten-speed bike.							
One day her Aunt Deb came to							
visit Mary's family. Aunt Deb							
heard that Mary wanted a new							
bike. She told Mary that she							
had some work for her. Mary							
walked over to Aunt Deb's house							
the very next day. Aunt Deb							
had Mary mop her kitchen floor.							
Mary cleaned out the flower beds.							
Mary swept out the carport. Finally							
Aunt Deb asked //							
Mary to fold her clean clothes.							
TOTALS							

Notes:

Examiner's Summary of Miscue Patterns:

PART III: DEVELOPMENTAL/PERFORMANCE SUMMARY

Silent Reading Comprehension

_____ 0–1 questions missed = Easy

_____ 2 questions missed = Adequate

_____ 3+ questions missed = Too hard

Oral Reading Accuracy

_____ 0–1 oral errors = Easy

_____ 2–5 oral errors = Adequate

_____ 6+ oral errors = Too hard

Continue to next assessment level passage? _____ Yes _____ No

Examiner's Notes:

Bedtime (246 words)

PART I: SILENT READING COMPREHENSION

Background Statement: "This is a story about a girl who has to go to bed. As you read the story, try to find out why she has to go to bed. Read it carefully because I'm going to ask you to tell me about it."

Teacher Directions: Once the student completes the silent reading, say, "Tell me about the story you just read." Check off any answers to the questions below that the student provides during the retelling. Ask all remaining questions not addressed during the retelling.

Questions/Answers	*Story Grammar Element/ Level of Comprehension*
_____1. Who were the people in the story? *(Wild Willie, Beth, and her Mother)*	character-characterization/ literal
_____2. Where was Wild Willie? *(the desert)*	setting/inferential
_____3. What was Wild Willie's problem? *(he was being followed)*	story problem(s)/literal
_____4. Why didn't Beth find out what was following Wild Willie? *(TV was turned off)*	story problem(s)/literal
_____5. How is Beth going to find out what was following Wild Willie? *(watch the reruns)*	problem resolution attempts/ inferential
_____6. If you were Beth, what other way can you think of to find out what was following Wild Willie? *(ask a friend, or any other plausible response)*	problem resolution/ inferential
_____7. How would you describe Beth's feelings when she had to go to bed? *(disappointed, mad, upset, or other plausible response)*	character-characterization/ evaluative
_____8. What were the two reasons Beth's Mother gave for shutting off the TV? *(it was a school day and it was getting late)*	problem resolution attempts/ literal

PART II: ORAL READING AND ANALYSIS OF MISCUES

Directions: Say, "Now I would like to hear you read this story out loud." Have the student read orally until the 100-word sample is completed. Follow along on the Miscue Grid, marking any oral reading errors as appropriate. *Remember to count miscues only up to the point in the story containing the oral reading stop-marker (//).* Then complete the Developmental/Performance Summary to determine whether to continue the assessment. *(Note:* The Miscue Grid should be completed *after* the assessment session has been concluded in order to minimize stress for the student.)

	MIS-PRONUN.	SUB-STITUTION	OMISSION	INSERTION	TCHR. ASSIST.	SELF-CORRECT.	MEANING DISRUPTION
Bedtime							
The sun was going down.							
The air was hot and Wild Willie							
was afraid. Never had he been							
in such a dry, hot place. His							
horse, Wizard, was trying to find							
a few blades of grass. Wild Willie							
was beginning to fall asleep							
from staying awake so long. Then							
he heard the sound again—the							
same sound he had been hearing for							
days. What could it be?							
Why was it following him? How							
could he find out what or who							
it was? Slowly Wizard turned							
around. Willie stood up in							
the stirrups to see over							
the sand dune. He							
saw // *no one.*							
TOTALS							

Notes:

Examiner's Summary of Miscue Patterns:

PART III: DEVELOPMENTAL/PERFORMANCE SUMMARY

Silent Reading Comprehension   **Oral Reading Accuracy**

_____ 0–1 questions missed = Easy   _____ 0–1 oral errors = Easy

_____ 2   questions missed = Adequate   _____ 2–5 oral errors = Adequate

_____ 3+   questions missed = Too hard   _____ 6+   oral errors = Too hard

Continue to next assessment level passage?   _____ Yes   _____ No

Examiner's Notes:

FORM B: LEVEL 4 ASSESSMENT PROTOCOLS

A Different Time (294 words)

PART I: SILENT READING COMPREHENSION

Background Statement: "This story is about a boy who lived a long time ago. Read the story to find out what Marlo wanted and why he couldn't have it. Read it carefully because I will ask you to tell me about it when you finish."

Teacher Directions: Once the student completes the silent reading, say, "Tell me about the story you just read." Check off any answers to the questions below that the student provides during the retelling. Ask all remaining questions not addressed during the retelling.

Questions/Answers   *Story Grammar Element/ Level of Comprehension*

_____1. Where did Marlo live?   setting/literal
(*in a hut*)

_____2. What was Marlo's problem?   story problem(s)/literal
(*he wanted to read*)

_____3. What did Marlo do that caused the old   problem resolution attempts/
man to help him?   inferential
(*gave him some vegetables*)

_____4. Where did Marlo have to meet the old man?   setting/literal
(*old oak tree*)

_____5. How was Marlo's problem solved?   problem resolution attempts/
(*the old man gave him a book so he could*   inferential
learn to read)

_____6. How would you describe Marlo?   character-characterization/
(*kind, nice, thankful, other plausible response*)   evaluative

_____7. How do you know that this story took place   setting/inferential
in olden times and not today?
(*castle, they lived in hut, used a cart, lots of people*
couldn't read, and other plausible responses)

_____8. Why is "be kind to others and they'll be kind   theme/evaluative
to you" a good theme for this story?
(*responses will vary but should indicate that*
Marlo got his wish because of his kindness)

PART II: ORAL READING AND ANALYSIS OF MISCUES

Directions: Say, "Now I would like to hear you read this story out loud." Have the student read orally until the 100-word sample is completed. Follow along on the Miscue Grid, marking any oral reading errors as appropriate. *Remember to count miscues only up to the point in the story containing the oral reading stop-marker (//).* Then complete the Developmental/Performance Summary to determine whether to continue the assessment. (*Note:* The Miscue Grid should be completed *after* the assessment session has been concluded in order to minimize stress for the student.)

	MIS-PRONUN.	SUB-STITUTION	OMISSION	INSERTION	TCHR. ASSIST.	SELF-CORRECT.	MEANING DISRUPTION
A Different Time							
Marlo lived in a different time							
and a different place. He lived							
in a time of darkness and gloom.							
Marlo lived in a small hut with							
his poor parents. He didn't have							
nice clothes and he didn't have							
much to eat. But neither of these							
things bothered Marlo. There was							
only one thing he wanted. But							
he couldn't have it because the							
ruler would not let any of							
his people have it. This most							
important thing was to be able							
to read. Today this may							
seem like a dumb wish, but to							
Marlo it wasn't. One day							
Marlo's father sent // *him*							
to the castle with a cart of vegetables.							
TOTALS							

Notes:

Examiner's Summary of Miscue Patterns:

PART III: DEVELOPMENTAL/PERFORMANCE SUMMARY

Silent Reading Comprehension

_____ 0–1 questions missed = Easy

_____ 2 questions missed = Adequate

_____ 3+ questions missed = Too hard

Continue to next assessment level passage? _____ Yes _____ No

Oral Reading Accuracy

_____ 0–1 oral errors = Easy

_____ 2–5 oral errors = Adequate

_____ 6+ oral errors = Too hard

Examiner's Notes:

FORM B: LEVEL 5 ASSESSMENT PROTOCOLS

Afternoon Walk (390 words)

PART I: SILENT READING COMPREHENSION

Background Statement: "This story is about a young girl who goes walking in woods that are sup-posed to be haunted. Read the story to find out what happens to Allison when she ventures into the haunted woods. Read it carefully because I will ask you to tell me about it when you finish."

Teacher Directions: Once the student completes the silent reading, say, "Tell me about the story you just read." Check off any answers to the questions below that the student provides during the retelling. Ask all remaining questions not addressed during the retelling.

Questions/Answers	*Story Grammar Element/ Level of Comprehension*
_____1. Who is the main character in this story? *(Allison)*	character-characterization/ literal
_____2. Where was Allison when she first met the old lady? *(in the woods or under an elm tree)*	setting/literal
_____3. Where did the old woman take Allison? *(to the old woman's hut)*	setting/literal
_____4. What was Allison's problem with the old woman? *(getting away before being sold to the dwarf or not acting tired)*	story problem(s)/inferential
_____5. How did Allison escape from the old woman? *(she ran out the door while the woman was looking for her dog)*	problem resolution/literal
_____6. What happened after Allison couldn't run any farther and fell asleep? *(her brother woke her up)*	problem resolution attempts/ literal
_____7. What happened after Allison was safely back home? *(she found a small metal tag with "Spirit" printed on it)*	problem resolution attempts/ literal
_____8. Why, in the story, did Allison always tell the old woman that she was not tired? *(because she didn't want to be sold)*	problem resolution attempts/ inferential

PART II: ORAL READING AND ANALYSIS OF MISCUES

Directions: Say, "Now I would like to hear you read this story out loud." Have the student read orally until the 100-word sample is completed. Follow along on the Miscue Grid, marking any oral reading errors as appropriate. *Remember to count miscues only up to the point in the story contain-ing the oral reading stop-marker (//).* Then complete the Developmental/Performance Summary to determine whether to continue the assessment. (*Note:* The Miscue Grid should be completed *after* the assessment session has been concluded in order to minimize stress for the student.)

	MIS-PRONUN.	SUB-STITUTION	OMISSION	INSERTION	TCHR. ASSIST.	SELF-CORRECT.	MEANING DISRUPTION
Afternoon Walk							
One day Allison was walking in							
the woods behind her house. Some of							
the other children in the neighborhood							
liked to tease her by saying that the							
woods were haunted. "There's an							
old, withered, witch-like woman							
in those woods who comes							
out at two o'clock every day to							
catch children," they'd say.							
"She makes them do housework							
and things like that. Then							
she sells them to a grim looking							
dwarf from far away when they are							
too tired to work. Once captured they							
are never seen again." Allison knew her							
friends were only telling stories,							
but it still frightened //							
her sometimes when she went							
into the woods.							
TOTALS							

Notes:

Examiner's Summary of Miscue Patterns:

PART III: DEVELOPMENTAL/PERFORMANCE SUMMARY

Silent Reading Comprehension

_____ 0–1 questions missed = Easy

_____ 2   questions missed = Adequate

_____ 3+   questions missed = Too hard

Oral Reading Accuracy

_____ 0–1 oral errors = Easy

_____ 2–5 oral errors = Adequate

_____ 6+   oral errors = Too hard

Continue to next assessment level passage?   _____ Yes   _____ No

Examiner's Notes:

Laser Boy (379 words)

PART I: SILENT READING COMPREHENSION

Background Statement: "This story is about a boy who had problems in school. Read the story to find out how the boy's problems were solved. Read it carefully because I'm going to ask you to tell me about it when you finish."

Teacher Directions: Once the student completes the silent reading, say, "Tell me about the story you just read." Check off any answers to the questions below that the student provides during the retelling. Ask all remaining questions not addressed during the retelling.

Questions/Answers	*Story Grammar Element/ Level of Comprehension*
_____1. Who was the story mainly about? *(Matthew)*	character-characterization/ literal
_____2. What was Matthew's problem? *(he wasn't doing well in school, or other plausible response)*	story problem(s)/inferential
_____3. What did Matthew's teacher decide to do about Matthew's problem? *(have Matthew tested for a learning problem)*	problem resolution attempts/ literal
_____4. Summarize what the school found out about Matthew's problem. *(he was gifted in math and science)*	problem resolution/inferential
_____5. How did the school try to solve the problem? *(it allowed Matthew to study what interested him the most)*	problem resolution attempts/ inferential
_____6. How was Matthew affected by being allowed to study what most interested him? *(he improved as a student and made friends)*	character-characterization/ inferential
_____7. How did Matthew's story affect the writer of this story? *(the writer believes everyone has special talents if you look for them)*	theme/evaluative
_____8. Why were the phone calls with the professor set up for Matthew? *(so he could ask the professor about lasers when he needed to)*	problem resolution attempts/ literal

PART II: ORAL READING AND ANALYSIS OF MISCUES

Directions: Say, "Now I would like to hear you read this story out loud." Have the student read orally until the 100-word sample is completed. Follow along on the Miscue Grid, marking any oral reading errors as appropriate. *Remember to count miscues only up to the point in the story containing the oral reading stop-marker (//).* Then complete the Developmental/Performance Summary to determine whether to continue the assessment. (*Note:* The Miscue Grid should be completed *after* the assessment session has been concluded in order to minimize stress for the student.)

	MIS-PRONUN.	SUB-STITUTION	OMISSION	INSERTION	TCHR. ASSIST.	SELF-CORRECT.	MEANING DISRUPTION
Laser Boy							
My name is Bob and I'm a teacher.							
Several years ago I knew a student							
that I'd like to tell you about.							
Matthew was a 13-year-old who never							
seemed to do well in school. Some							
say that he was a misfit, someone							
who doesn't quite fit in with the							
other kids his age.							
Not only that, Matthew							
had trouble in school nearly							
his whole life.							
He failed to complete his							
homework even when it was							
an easy assignment.							
By not participating in class,							
not turning in homework, and							
only doing a fair job on tests,							
Matthew always seemed							
to // *be just barely passing.*							
TOTALS							

Notes:

Examiner's Summary of Miscue Patterns:

PART III: DEVELOPMENTAL/PERFORMANCE SUMMARY

Silent Reading Comprehension

_____ 0–1 questions missed = Easy

_____ 2 questions missed = Adequate

_____ 3+ questions missed = Too hard

Oral Reading Accuracy

_____ 0–1 oral errors = Easy

_____ 2–5 oral errors = Adequate

_____ 6+ oral errors = Too hard

Continue to next assessment level passage? _____ Yes _____ No

Examiner's Notes:

FORM B: LEVEL 7 ASSESSMENT PROTOCOLS

The Paper Route (435 words)

PART I: SILENT READING COMPREHENSION

Background Statement: "This story is about a boy who begins his first job as a paperboy. Read it to find out what his first year as a paperboy was like. Read it carefully because I will ask you to tell me about it when you finish."

Teacher Directions: Once the student completes the silent reading, say, "Tell me about the story you just read." Check off any answers to the questions below that the student provides during the retelling. Ask all remaining questions not addressed during the retelling.

Questions/Answers	*Story Grammar Element/ Level of Comprehension*
_____ 1. Who were the main characters in the story? *(Scott and Mr. Miley)*	character-characterization/ literal
_____ 2. How did Scott get a chance to earn money? *(by answering an ad for newspaper carriers)*	problem resolution attempts/ literal
_____ 3. What did Scott have to do each morning after picking up his newspapers? *(roll them and put them in plastic bags)*	problem resolution attempts/ literal
_____ 4. Why were Thursdays and Sundays problems for Scott? *(papers were extra large and it took many trips to get them delivered)*	story problem(s)/inferential
_____ 5. What were the two main problems Scott faced with his job? *(bad weather and cranky customers)*	story problem(s)/literal
_____ 6. How did Scott handle the problem of cranky customers? *(by going out of his way to please them)*	problem resolution/literal
_____ 7. What words would you use to describe Scott? *(responses will vary but should reflect the idea of hardworking, conscientious)*	character-characterization/ evaluative
_____ 8. What lessons would a job like Scott's teach? *(responses will vary but should indicate a theme related to benefits of hard work)*	theme/evaluative

PART II: ORAL READING AND ANALYSIS OF MISCUES

Directions: Say, "Now I would like to hear you read this story out loud." Have the student read orally until the 100-word sample is completed. Follow along on the Miscue Grid, marking any oral reading errors as appropriate. *Remember to count miscues only up to the point in the story containing the oral reading stop-marker (//).* Then complete the Developmental/Performance Summary to determine whether to continue the assessment. (*Note:* The Miscue Grid should be completed *after* the assessment session has been concluded in order to minimize stress for the student.)

	MIS-PRONUN.	SUB-STITUTION	OMISSION	INSERTION	TCHR. ASSIST.	SELF-CORRECT.	MEANING DISRUPTION
The Paper Route							
Scott had a chance to earn his own							
money for the first time. Answering							
an advertisement for newspaper							
carriers, he set up an appointment							
with Mr. Miley, the distribution							
manager. Mr. Miley was a rather							
short and stocky man who spoke							
with a loud voice. After reviewing							
Scott's application, Mr. Miley							
said, "You look like a dependable							
young man to me. Do your							
parents approve of your becoming							
a paperboy?" "Yes, sir," replied							
Scott, "and I have a letter from							
my Dad saying it's OK with him."							
"You can have the job, Scott," said Mr.							
Miley. "However, I want you to //							
realize that this is a long route and							
you will have to get up very early.							
TOTALS							

Notes:

Examiner's Summary of Miscue Patterns:

PART III: DEVELOPMENTAL/PERFORMANCE SUMMARY

Silent Reading Comprehension   **Oral Reading Accuracy**

_____ 0–1 questions missed = Easy   _____ 0–1 oral errors = Easy

_____ 2   questions missed = Adequate   _____ 2–5 oral errors = Adequate

_____ 3+   questions missed = Too hard   _____ 6+   oral errors = Too hard

Continue to next assessment level passage?   _____ Yes   _____ No

Examiner's Notes:

Riley and Leonard (430 words)

PART I: SILENT READING COMPREHENSION

Background Statement: "This is a story about a boy named Leonard who was very unpopular in school. Read this story to find out how Leonard deals with his problem. Read it carefully because I'm going to ask you to tell me about it when you finish."

Teacher Directions: Once the student completes the silent reading, say, "Tell me about the story you just read." Check off any answers to the questions below that the student provides during the retelling. Ask all remaining questions not addressed during the retelling.

Questions/Answers	Story Grammar Element/ Level of Comprehension
_____1. Who were the main characters in the story? *(Leonard, Riley, Lorrie)*	character-characterization/ literal
_____2. What was Leonard's problem when he was in school? *(he was unpopular)*	story problem(s)/literal
_____3. What problem resolution attempts did Leonard make when his fellow students made negative comments about his family? *(he started a fight)*	problem resolution attempts/ literal
_____4. How did the fight end? *(Leonard was forced to give up; he lost)*	problem resolution attempts/ literal
_____5. How did Leonard solve his problem of being unpopular? *(by becoming successful and involved in civic projects)*	problem resolution/ inferential
_____6. Where did the accident take place? *(outside the fancy restaurant)*	setting/literal
_____7. What caused the beggar to step into the path of the truck? *(surprise at both the amount of money and the fact that it was Leonard)*	problem resolution attempts/ inferential
_____8. What is the theme/moral of this passage? *(responses will vary but should indicate a theme/ moral related to "what goes around comes around")*	theme/evaluative

PART II: ORAL READING AND ANALYSIS OF MISCUES

Directions: Say, "Now I would like to hear you read this story out loud." Have the student read orally until the 100-word sample is completed. Follow along on the Miscue Grid, marking any oral reading errors as appropriate. *Remember to count miscues only up to the point in the story containing the oral reading stop-marker (//).* Then complete the Developmental/Performance Summary to determine whether to continue the assessment. (*Note:* The Miscue Grid should be completed *after* the assessment session has been concluded in order to minimize stress for the student.)

	MIS-PRONUN.	SUB-STITUTION	OMISSION	INSERTION	TCHR. ASSIST.	SELF-CORRECT.	MEANING DISRUPTION
Riley and Leonard							
At times Leonard felt like							
the most unpopular boy in school.							
No matter what he did he was							
constantly ridiculed by his classmates.							
Maybe it was because he was							
small in stature and wore thick							
bifocals. Or maybe it was							
because he didn't like sports. Possibly							
it was because he couldn't afford							
the designer clothes the other kids							
seemed to live for. Regardless, Leonard							
felt like a loser and was unhappy							
with his situation. One day, while							
putting his books in his locker,							
the familiar mockery began. A							
small covey of classmates formed a							
semicircle around Leonard. Each							
began to taunt // *him*							
and call him names.							
TOTALS							

Notes:

Examiner's Summary of Miscue Patterns:

PART III: DEVELOPMENTAL/PERFORMANCE SUMMARY

Silent Reading Comprehension

_____ 0–1 questions missed = Easy

_____ 2   questions missed = Adequate

_____ 3+   questions missed = Too hard

Continue to next assessment level passage?   _____ Yes   _____ No

Oral Reading Accuracy

_____ 0–1 oral errors = Easy

_____ 2–5 oral errors = Adequate

_____ 6+   oral errors = Too hard

Examiner's Notes:

The Long Night (474 words)

PART I: SILENT READING COMPREHENSION

Background Statement: "This story is about mistaken identity. Read it carefully because I will ask you to tell me about the story when you finish reading."

Teacher Directions: Once the student completes the silent reading, say, "Tell me about the story you just read." Check off any answers to the questions below that the student provides during the retelling. Ask all remaining questions not addressed during the retelling.

Questions/Answers

Story Grammar Element/ Level of Comprehension

_____1. Where and at what time of day did this story take place?
(*nighttime in New Orleans*)

setting/literal

_____2. What was the problem facing the writer
of this story while he walked up Rampart?
(*he was being followed and someone gave him
a note that said he was going to die*)

story problem(s)/inferential

_____3. How did the policeman react to his story?
(*didn't really believe him*)

problem resolution attempts/
literal

_____4. What happened after he left the policeman?
(*he was taken into a building by two men*)

problem resolution attempts/
literal

_____5. How did the writer of this story solve the problem(s)?
(*it turned out to be a case of mistaken identity*)

problem resolution/
inferential

_____6. Who was Nero, and how would you describe him?
(*he was the boss, a criminal, and a nasty kind
of character*)

character-characterization/
inferential

_____7. What series of events got the person in this
story into such trouble?
(*flight delay, walking alone at night, and he looked
like someone else*)

story problem(s)/inferential

_____8. What did the author do after he was released?
(*stayed two more days and never returned*)

problem resolution attempts/
literal

PART II: ORAL READING AND ANALYSIS OF MISCUES

Directions: Say, "Now I would like to hear you read this story out loud." Have the student read orally until the 100-word sample is completed. Follow along on the Miscue Grid, marking any oral reading errors as appropriate. *Remember to count miscues only up to the point in the story containing the oral reading stop-marker (//).* Then complete the Developmental/Performance Summary to determine whether to continue the assessment. (*Note:* The Miscue Grid should be completed *after* the assessment session has been concluded in order to minimize stress for the student.)

	MIS-PRONUN.	SUB-STITUTION	OMISSION	INSERTION	TCHR. ASSIST.	SELF-CORRECT.	MEANING DISRUPTION
The Long Night							
I arrived late at the New Orleans							
International Airport because of							
delays in St. Louis. The night							
was descending on the							
Crescent City as I entered							
the cab for the short ride to							
city center. As the cab headed							
toward the city, the cabbie engaged							
me in an informative conversation							
about the Crescent City. She had an							
island accent and her multicolored							
dress was very nontraditional.							
After I told her I wanted to							
go to Rampart in the							
French Quarter, she abruptly turned							
left and headed southwest.							
Fifteen minutes later, without a word,							
I got out of the cab // *and proceeded*							
up Rampart.							
TOTALS							

Notes:

Examiner's Summary of Miscue Patterns:

PART III: DEVELOPMENTAL/PERFORMANCE SUMMARY

Silent Reading Comprehension

_____ 0–1 questions missed = Easy

_____ 2 questions missed = Adequate

_____ 3+ questions missed = Too hard

Continue to next assessment level passage?   _____ Yes   _____ No

Oral Reading Accuracy

_____ 0–1 oral errors = Easy

_____ 2–5 oral errors = Adequate

_____ 6+ oral errors = Too hard

Examiner's Notes:

FORM C
Sentences for Initial Passage Selection

FORM C: LEVEL 1

1. Some animals are fun.

2. I eat lots of food.

3. He can smell good.

FORM C: LEVEL 2

1. It was a very clear night.

2. I get hot when the sun shines bright.

3. We can't see air moving.

FORM C: LEVEL 3

1. Many insects are very helpful.

2. Some adults are slender, some are fat.

3. I agree that it is the most beautiful flower.

FORM C: LEVEL 4

1. A famous man would know what to do.

2. The invention was very important.

3. Instead of jam I like syrup on my food.

FORM C: LEVEL 5

1. The estimate for my car was not acceptable.

2. Various people came immediately to the fire.

3. The amount of water you drink is important.

FORM C: LEVEL 6

1. He considered it carefully, but it was too expensive.

2. The new method of raising the temperature got good results.

3. What is common today is the result of many years of experimenting.

FORM C: LEVEL 7

1. Scientists hope to transform the industrial site before the end of the year.

2. Foreign minerals are used to develop usable compounds.

3. The presence of impurities lowers the value of all gems.

FORM C: LEVEL 8

1. Scientists are always looking for advancements to improve the world.

2. The prearranged site was eliminated.

3. To compress hundreds of wires into one is called "fiber optics."

FORM C: LEVEL 9

1. He moved in a circular motion, then ran off laterally.

2. The vertical object couldn't be viewed easily.

3. At the intersection, a series of accidents occurred.

FORM C
Expository Passages

Bears

There are many kinds of bears.

Some bears are brown. Others are black.

Still others are white and are called polar bears.

The biggest bears are called grizzly bears.

Bears can smell and hear very well.

Bears have small eyes and cannot see very well.

They eat all kinds of food.

They eat small animals, plants, and berries.

Most bears sleep during the winter.

When they wake up they are hungry.

Bears can run very fast.

They can climb trees.

They are not safe animals to be around.

The best place to be around bears is at the zoo.

The Night Sky

Look up at the sky at night. If it is a clear night, you will see stars. How many stars are there? No one knows for sure. But there is one star that you know by name. You can see it in the daytime. It is our sun. The sun is a star. All stars are suns. Our sun is so close that we cannot see other stars in the day. We only see the other suns at night.

Stars are made up of very hot gas and they seem to twinkle because of the air moving across them. Even though we can't always see them, they are always in the sky, even in the daytime.

Flying Flowers

There are many kinds of insects. There are big ones, little ones, ugly ones, biting ones, and helpful ones. But there is one kind of insect that most people agree is the most beautiful one. This insect is often called the flying flower. It is the butterfly.

Butterflies are insects that have two pairs of wings. The wings are covered with tiny scales. The scales are different colors. These scales give the butterfly its beautiful colors. Butterflies smell and hear by using their long, thin antennae. Butterflies can't bite or chew. They use long, tube-like tongues to get at the food they eat from flowers.

Butterflies begin as eggs. Then they hatch into caterpillars. A caterpillar forms a hard skin. When they finally break out of the hard skin, they are butterflies with colorful wings. Adult butterflies must lay eggs soon. They do not live very long.

Butterflies and moths are different. Butterflies like the day. Moths like the night. Moths are not as colorful as butterflies. Butterfly bodies are slender, while moths tend to have large, fat bodies. Moths form cocoons before turning into winged insects. Most butterflies do not form cocoons.

The Story of Coca-Cola

Lots of people all over the world have heard of the soft drink called Coca-Cola. But not many people know the real story about how this drink was invented.

Coca-Cola was the invention of a Mr. John Pemberton. Although he wasn't a doctor, most people called him Dr. Pemberton. He was a druggist in a town in the South. Dr. Pemberton liked to invent new things. He lived during the time just after the Civil War.

One day Dr. Pemberton decided to make a headache medicine. He made it from nuts, fruits, and leaves. He also added the drugs necessary to cure a headache. Dr. Pemberton now thought he had something to sell that tasted good.

In the summer of 1886, Dr. Pemberton took a jug of this headache syrup to one of the best drugstores in Atlanta, Georgia. He told the manager of the drugstore to mix some of the syrup with water and have just people with headaches drink it. At first it did not sell very well. Then one day a clerk sold some of the new medicine to a customer with a bad headache. But instead of using regular water, he used carbonated water by accident. Carbonated water has bubbles in it. Everyone loved this new change, and carbonated water is still used in Coca-Cola today.

Most of the medicine that cures headaches was taken out of Coca-Cola as time went on. But Dr. Pemberton's drink is still one of the world's favorite soft drinks.

Popcorn

There are three major types of corn grown in this country. First, there is the type of corn people eat most of the time. It is called sweet corn because of its flavor. Second, there is field corn, which is used mainly for feeding livestock. Sometimes people eat field corn too. However, its taste is not as good as sweet corn and its kernels are not as full. The third type of corn, often called Indian corn, is popcorn. Popcorn is grown commercially in the United States because the average American eats almost two pounds of popcorn a year, according to various estimates.

When America was discovered by Columbus, Native Americans had been eating popcorn for thousands of years. They prepared it several different ways. One way was to stick the ear of corn on a stick and place it over a campfire. Any kernels that popped out of the fire were gathered up and eaten. Another method was to scrape the cob and throw the kernels into the fire. Any kernels that popped out of the fire were immediately eaten. Since these methods limited how many kernels could actually be eaten, the Native Americans began to use small clay bowls that they would heat sand in. When the sand got really hot, they placed the popcorn in the bowls and waited for the kernels to pop.

Popcorn is popcorn because of the amount of water content of the kernel. Most experts agree that, ideally, a kernel should have at least fourteen percent water content to be good corn for popping. If the corn kernels have less than twelve percent water content, then the kernels will be duds. They won't pop right.

Cooking Without Fire: The Microwave Oven

Microwave cooking is very common today. It is, however, a recent invention. The microwave oven one uses today was developed from the invention of the magnetron tube in 1940. The invention of the magnetron tube, by Sir John Randall and Dr. H. A. Boot, was a very important part of the radar defense of England during World War II. Neither man considered it as a means of preparing food after they invented it.

It wasn't until the late 1940s that Dr. Percy Spencer discovered the magnetron's ability to heat and cook food from the inside out. Spencer experimented with many different foods, all with the same results: The inside got hot first.

It took several years for the company Spencer worked for to develop what we know today as the microwave oven. Not until around 1952 could a person purchase a microwave oven, then called a Radar Range, for home use. These early models were expensive and bulky.

Today's microwave ovens are inexpensive and come with a variety of features. The features include: defrost, constant temperature cooking, and automatic reheat. Microwave cooking, many claim, was the first completely new method of cooking food since early humans discovered fire. Why? Because microwave cooking requires no fire or element of fire to cook food. The food is cooked by electromagnetic energy.

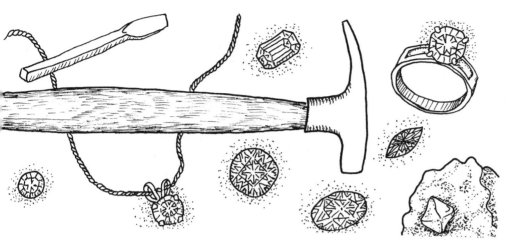

Diamonds

A diamond is one of the most beautiful treasures that nature ever created, and one of the rarest. It takes thousands of years for nature to transform a chunk of carbon into a rough diamond. Only three important diamond fields have been found in the world—in India, South America, and Africa.

The first diamonds were found in the sand and gravel of stream beds. These types of diamonds are called alluvial diamonds. Later, diamonds were found deep in the earth in rock formations called pipes. These formations resemble extinct volcanoes. The rock in which diamonds are found is called blue ground. Yet even where diamonds are plentiful, it takes digging and sorting through tons of rock and gravel to find enough diamonds for a one-carat ring.

Gem diamonds' quality is based on weight, purity, color, and cut. The weight of a diamond is measured by the carat. Its purity is determined by the presence or absence of impurities, such as foreign minerals and uncrystallized carbon. The color of diamonds varies, but most diamonds are tinged yellow or brown. The cut of a diamond also figures into its value. A fully cut diamond, often called flawless, would have fifty-eight facets. Facets, or sides, cause the brilliance that is produced when a diamond is struck by light.

Humans have learned how to make artificial diamonds. Manufactured diamonds are placed in a machine that creates the same pressure that exists about two hundred and fifty miles beneath the surface of the earth. Besides intense pressure, the carbon compounds are heated to temperatures over five thousand degrees Fahrenheit. Unfortunately, the created diamonds are small and are used mainly in industrial settings. They have no value as gems.

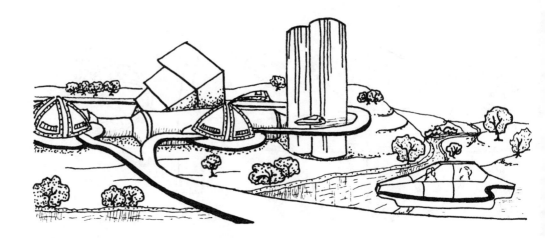

The Future Is Here

What will the twenty-first century bring in terms of new inventions and space-age technologies? No one knows for sure. But scientists, inventors, and futurists are predicting a variety of new inventions. These new advancements will affect the way we live and play. Some of them are already on the drawing board.

One example is the levitation vehicle. The idea of a vertical take-off and landing aircraft that can also be driven on the road is the invention of Paul Moeller. He named his version of this type of craft the Moeller 400. People involved in this type of technology see increases in population and crowded highways as reasons that a levitation vehicle will be needed. Imagine flying into the city, hovering over a prearranged landing site, landing, and then driving the rest of the way to work.

Another innovation that will be refined during the 1990s is the dental laser. Researchers have developed a laser that they hope will replace the much feared dental drill. The laser basically vaporizes the cavity without affecting the surrounding enamel. As a bonus, the laser will eliminate the need of a shot for deadening surrounding tissue.

Probably one of the most significant new technologies that will affect people in the near future is the advent of fiber optics. Fiber optics compress hundreds of wires into one, thus allowing for the communication of huge amounts of information over very thin wires. One example of the application of fiber optics will be the development of full-motion, color video telephones. These will be particularly important to the deaf.

Another advancement that is on the horizon is high-definition television. The average consumer will be able to upgrade his or her current televiewing dramatically when high-definition television becomes widely available. The color of these televisions will have the vividness of 35-millimeter movies and the sound quality of compact discs. This refinement will lead to improvements in at-home movies and video games, both of which will be available in three-dimensional formats.

Regardless of new advancements in technology, people must be prepared to face the challenges of the future: namely, to assist each other as we travel through time, and to help preserve our home, the earth.

Visual Illusions

A visual illusion is an unreal or misleading appearance or image, according to *Webster's* dictionary. In other words, visual illusions are sometimes caused by ideas one holds about what one expects to see. In other instances, the illusion is caused by the brain's difficulty in choosing from two or more visual patterns.

If you look at a bull's-eye and move it slowly in circular motions, you should see spokes moving. The spokes, if you see them, aren't really there. This type of visual illusion is called lateral inhibition.

Another type of visual illusion occurs when a person tries to estimate the height of a vertical object. It is referred to as length distortion. The famous Gateway Arch in St. Louis is an example of length distortion, because the arch seems much higher than it is wide. In reality the height and width of the arch are identical. Length distortion occurs because our eyes move more easily from side to side than up and down. This greater effort to look up causes the brain to over-interpret the height of vertical objects.

If you look at a series of squares, you should see small gray spots at each intersection. If you look directly at one intersection the spots should disappear. This illusion is known as Hermann's Grid. It is often seen in modern high-rise office buildings. Many of these buildings have windows separated by crossing strips of metal or concrete.

The above are only three examples of the many ways that our eyes can deceive us. But they do reinforce the old axiom, "Don't believe everything you see."

FORM C

Examiner's Assessment Protocols

FORM C: LEVEL 1 ASSESSMENT PROTOCOLS

Bears (99 words)

PART I: SILENT READING COMPREHENSION

Background Statement: "This story is about bears. Read this story to find out information about the different kinds of bears. Read it carefully because I'm going to ask you to tell me about what you read."

Teacher Directions: Once the student completes the silent reading, say, "Why don't you tell me what you found out about bears?" Check off any answers to the questions below that the student provides during the retelling. Ask all remaining questions not addressed during the retelling.

Questions/Answers	*Expository Grammar Element/ Level of Comprehension*
_____ 1. What kinds of bears did you read about? *(brown, black, polar, and grizzly)*	collection/literal
_____ 2. What kind of bear is the biggest of all? *(grizzly bear)*	description/literal
_____ 3. Explain why bears are not safe to be around. *(plausible responses related to they are wild animals, don't like humans, can run fast and climb trees)*	problem resolution attempts/ inferential
_____ 4. What are some things bears can do very well? *(smell, hear, run, climb—any three)*	collection/literal
_____ 5. How do bears find their food? *(smelling and hearing)*	problem resolution attempts/ inferential
_____ 6. Why are bears often hungry after winter? *(because they sleep most of the winter)*	causation/inferential
_____ 7. Can you name two things that bears eat? *(plants, berries, and small animals)*	collection/literal
_____ 8. Where did the story say was the best place to be around bears? *(at the zoo)*	description/literal

PART II: ORAL READING AND ANALYSIS OF MISCUES

Directions: Say, "Now I would like to hear you read this story out loud." Have the student read orally until the passage is completed. Follow along on the Miscue Grid, marking any oral reading errors as appropriate. Then complete the Developmental/Performance Summary to determine whether to continue the assessment. (*Note:* The Miscue Grid should be completed *after* the assessment session has been concluded in order to minimize stress for the student.)

	MIS-PRONUN.	SUB-STITUTION	OMISSION	INSERTION	TCHR. ASSIST.	SELF-CORRECT.	MEANING DISRUPTION
Bears							
There are many kinds of bears.							
Some bears are brown. Others are							
black. Still others are white and							
are called polar bears. The biggest							
bears are called grizzly bears.							
Bears can smell and hear very							
well. Bears have small eyes and							
cannot see very well. They eat all							
kinds of food. They eat							
small animals, plants, and							
berries. Most bears sleep during							
the winter. When they wake up							
they are hungry. Bears can run							
very fast. They can climb trees.							
They are not safe animals to							
be around. The best place							
to be around bears is							
at the zoo. //							
TOTALS							

Notes:

Examiner's Summary of Miscue Patterns:

PART III: DEVELOPMENTAL/PERFORMANCE SUMMARY

Silent Reading Comprehension

_____ 0–1 questions missed = Easy

_____ 2   questions missed = Adequate

_____ 3+   questions missed = Too hard

Oral Reading Accuracy

_____ 0–1 oral errors = Easy

_____ 2–5 oral errors = Adequate

_____ 6+   oral errors = Too hard

Continue to next assessment level passage?   _____ Yes   _____ No

Examiner's Notes:

FORM C: LEVEL 2 ASSESSMENT PROTOCOLS

The Night Sky (116 words)

PART I: SILENT READING COMPREHENSION

Background Statement: "This story is about stars. Read it and try to remember some of the important facts about stars because I'm going to ask you to tell me about what you have read."

Teacher Directions: Once the student completes the silent reading, say, "Tell me what you found out about stars." Check off any answers to the questions below that the student provides during the retelling. Ask any questions not answered during the retelling.

Questions/Answers	*Expository Grammar Element/ Level of Comprehension*
_____1. What kind of night is best for seeing stars? (*clear night*)	description/literal
_____2. What are stars made of? (*hot gases*)	description/literal
_____3. What star can you see only in the daytime? (*the sun*)	causation/literal
_____4. What causes stars to twinkle? (*the air moving across them*)	causation/literal
_____5. Why can't people on earth see other stars during the day? (*the sun is so close and bright*)	collection/literal
_____6. If one night you looked up at the sky and could see no stars, what could be the reason? (*cloudy night*)	problem resolution attempts/ evaluative
_____7. Explain why saying "look at all the suns in the night sky" is not a wrong statement. (*because all stars are suns*)	causation/literal
_____8. Can you name one reason why the earth cannot be called a star? (*it is not made up of hot gases, it is a planet not a star, it has water, and any other plausible responses*)	comparison/evaluative

PART II: ORAL READING AND ANALYSIS OF MISCUES

Directions: Say, "Now I would like to hear you read this story out loud." Have the student read orally until the 100-word sample is completed. Follow along on the Miscue Grid, marking any oral reading errors as appropriate. *Remember to count miscues only up to the point in the story containing the oral reading stop-marker (//).* Then complete the Developmental/Performance Summary to determine whether to continue the assessment. (*Note:* The Miscue Grid should be completed *after* the assessment session has been concluded in order to minimize stress for the student.)

	MIS-PRONUN.	SUB-STITUTION	OMISSION	INSERTION	TCHR. ASSIST.	SELF-CORRECT.	MEANING DISRUPTION
The Night Sky							
Look up at the sky at night.							
If it is a clear night, you will							
see stars. How many stars are							
there? No one knows for							
sure. But there is one star that							
you know by name. You							
can see it in the daytime. It							
is our sun. The sun is a star.							
All stars are suns. Our sun							
is so close that we cannot see other							
stars in the day. We only see							
the other suns at night. Stars are							
made up of very hot gas and							
they seem to twinkle because of							
the air moving across them.							
Even // *though we can't always see*							
them, they are always in the sky,							
even in the daytime.							
TOTALS							

Notes:

Examiner's Summary of Miscue Patterns:

PART III: DEVELOPMENTAL/PERFORMANCE SUMMARY

Silent Reading Comprehension

_____ 0–1 questions missed = Easy

_____ 2   questions missed = Adequate

_____ 3+   questions missed = Too hard

Oral Reading Accuracy

_____ 0–1 oral errors = Easy

_____ 2–5 oral errors = Adequate

_____ 6+   oral errors = Too hard

Continue to next assessment level passage?   _____ Yes   _____ No

Examiner's Notes:

FORM C: LEVEL 3 ASSESSMENT PROTOCOLS

Flying Flowers (194 words)

PART I: SILENT READING COMPREHENSION

Background Statement: "This selection is about a special kind of insect. It is about butterflies. Read this selection to find out some interesting facts about butterflies. I will ask you to tell me about what you read, so read carefully."

Teacher Directions: Once the student completes the silent reading, say, "Tell me about what you just read." Check off any answers to the questions below that the student provides during the retelling. Ask all remaining questions not addressed during the retelling.

Questions/Answers	*Expository Grammar Element/ Level of Comprehension*
_____1. What kind of insect was the passage mainly about? *(butterfly)*	description/literal
_____2. Why is the butterfly referred to as the flying flower? *(because of its many different colors)*	collection/inferential
_____3. What gives the butterfly its colors? *(scales)*	causation/literal
_____4. Can you name two ways in which a butterfly and a moth are different? *(butterflies like the day, are more colorful, are thinner, and most don't form cocoons—moths are the opposite)*	comparison/literal
_____5. Can you name two ways in which a butterfly and a moth are alike? *(they fly, lay eggs, have scales, have wings, etc.)*	comparison/inferential
_____6. What are the antennae of a butterfly used for? *(to smell and hear)*	collection/literal
_____7. Why do grown-up butterflies have to lay eggs as soon as possible? *(they don't live very long)*	problem resolution attempts/ inferential
_____8. What happens after a butterfly egg becomes a caterpillar? *(it forms a hard skin that it has to break out of)*	causation/literal

PART II: ORAL READING AND ANALYSIS OF MISCUES

Directions: Say, "Now I would like to hear you read this story out loud." Have the student read orally until the 100-word sample is completed. Follow along on the Miscue Grid, marking any oral reading errors as appropriate. *Remember to count miscues only up to the point in the story containing the oral reading stop-marker (//).* Then complete the Developmental/Performance Summary to determine whether to continue the assessment. (*Note:* The Miscue Grid should be completed *after* the assessment session has been concluded in order to minimize stress for the student.)

	MIS-PRONUN.	SUB-STITUTION	OMISSION	INSERTION	TCHR. ASSIST.	SELF-CORRECT.	MEANING DISRUPTION
Flying Flowers							
There are many kinds of insects.							
There are big ones, little ones, ugly							
ones, biting ones, and helpful ones.							
But there is one kind of insect							
that most people agree is the most							
beautiful one. This insect is often							
called the flying flower. It is							
the butterfly. Butterflies are insects							
that have two pairs of wings.							
The wings are covered with tiny							
scales. The scales are different							
colors. These scales give the							
butterfly its beautiful colors.							
Butterflies smell and hear by using							
their long, thin antennae. Butterflies							
can't bite or chew. They use long,							
tube-like tongues to get at // *the food*							
they eat from flowers.							
TOTALS							

Notes:

Examiner's Summary of Miscue Patterns:

PART III: DEVELOPMENTAL/PERFORMANCE SUMMARY

Silent Reading Comprehension

_____ 0–1 questions missed = Easy

_____ 2 questions missed = Adequate

_____ 3+ questions missed = Too hard

Continue to next assessment level passage? _____ Yes _____ No

Oral Reading Accuracy

_____ 0–1 oral errors = Easy

_____ 2–5 oral errors = Adequate

_____ 6+ oral errors = Too hard

Examiner's Notes:

The Story of Coca-Cola (253 words)

PART I: SILENT READING COMPREHENSION

Background Statement: "This selection is about the history of Coca-Cola. Read it carefully and try to find out some facts about Coca-Cola, because I'm going to ask you to tell me about what you find."

Teacher Directions: Once the student completes the silent reading, say, "Tell me what you just read about Coca-Cola." Check off any answers to the questions below that the student provides during the retelling. Ask all remaining questions not addressed during the retelling.

Questions/Answers	*Expository Grammar Element/ Level of Comprehension*
_____1. Who invented Coca-Cola? *(Mr./Dr. Pemberton)*	causation/literal
_____2. What was Dr. Pemberton trying to invent when he invented Coca-Cola? *(headache medicine)*	description/literal
_____3. Besides drugs for headaches, what other things were put into Dr. Pemberton's new medicine? *(leaves, fruits, and nuts)*	description/literal
_____4. Why didn't the medicine sell very well at first? *(because the syrup was mixed with regular water)*	causation/inferential
_____5. Why could one say that Coca-Cola became popular because of a mistake? *(because a clerk accidentally mixed the syrup with carbonated water)*	problem resolution attempts/ inferential
_____6. In which city did the original Coca-Cola become a hit? *(Atlanta)*	description/literal
_____7. Explain what is different between today's Coca-Cola and the original version. *(no headache medicine, or other plausible response)*	comparison/inferential
_____8. What's the difference between regular water and carbonated water? *(regular water doesn't have bubbles in it)*	comparison/inferential

PART II: ORAL READING AND ANALYSIS OF MISCUES

Directions: Say, "Now I would like to hear you read this story out loud." Have the student read orally until the 100-word sample is completed. Follow along on the Miscue Grid, marking any oral reading errors as appropriate. *Remember to count miscues only up to the point in the story containing the oral reading stop-marker (//).* Then complete the Developmental/Performance Summary to determine whether to continue the assessment. (*Note:* The Miscue Grid should be completed *after* the assessment session has been concluded in order to minimize stress for the student.)

	MIS-PRONUN.	SUB-STITUTION	OMISSION	INSERTION	TCHR. ASSIST.	SELF-CORRECT.	MEANING DISRUPTION
The Story of Coca-Cola							
Lots of people all over the world							
have heard of the soft drink							
called Coca-Cola. But not many							
people know the real story about							
how this drink was invented.							
Coca-Cola was the invention of							
a Mr. John Pemberton. Although he							
wasn't a doctor, most people called							
him Dr. Pemberton. He was a							
druggist in a town in the South.							
Dr. Pemberton liked to invent new							
things. He lived during the time							
just after the Civil War. One day							
Dr. Pemberton decided to make a							
headache medicine. He made it from							
nuts, fruits, and leaves. He also							
added the // *drugs necessary*							
to cure a headache.							
TOTALS							

Notes:

Examiner's Summary of Miscue Patterns:

PART III: DEVELOPMENTAL/PERFORMANCE SUMMARY

Silent Reading Comprehension

_____ 0–1 questions missed = Easy

_____ 2 questions missed = Adequate

_____ 3+ questions missed = Too hard

Oral Reading Accuracy

_____ 0–1 oral errors = Easy

_____ 2–5 oral errors = Adequate

_____ 6+ oral errors = Too hard

Continue to next assessment level passage? _____ Yes _____ No

Examiner's Notes:

▗▄▖ FORM C: LEVEL 5 ASSESSMENT PROTOCOLS ▗▄▖

Popcorn (282 words)

PART I: SILENT READING COMPREHENSION

Background Statement: "This selection is about corn, and *popcorn* in particular. Read the passage to discover some interesting facts about corn. Read it carefully because I'm going to ask you to tell me about what you read."

Teacher Directions: Once the student completes the silent reading, say, "Tell me about the story you just read." Check off any answers to the questions below that the student provides during the retelling. Ask all remaining questions not addressed during the retelling.

Questions/Answers	*Expository Grammar Element/ Level of Comprehension*
_____1. Which type of corn is this passage mainly about? *(Indian corn or popcorn)*	description/inferential
_____2. Explain how sweet corn differs from field corn. *(sweet corn is not used to feed livestock, tastes better, and has fuller kernels)*	comparison/inferential
_____3. What makes popcorn pop? *(water in the kernel)*	causation/inferential
_____4. What does the term *duds* mean when talking about popcorn? *(unpopped kernels)*	description/literal
_____5. Which of the methods to pop corn used by the Native Americans was the most effective, and why? *(the hot sand/clay bowl method because more kernels could be saved)*	problem resolution attempts/ inferential
_____6. How many pounds of popcorn did the passage say that the typical person in this country eats per year? *(two pounds)*	description/literal
_____7. How long did the passage say popcorn has been eaten by humans? *(thousands of years)*	description/literal
_____8. What is one limitation or problem associated with all three methods used by the Native Americans to pop corn? *(all lost kernels)*	problem resolution attempts/ inferential

PART II: ORAL READING AND ANALYSIS OF MISCUES

Directions: Say, "Now I would like to hear you read this story out loud." Have the student read orally until the 100-word sample is completed. Follow along on the Miscue Grid, marking any oral reading errors as appropriate. *Remember to count miscues only up to the point in the story containing the oral reading stop-marker (//).* Then complete the Developmental/Performance Summary to determine whether to continue the assessment. (*Note:* The Miscue Grid should be completed *after* the assessment session has been concluded in order to minimize stress for the student.)

	MIS-PRONUN.	SUB-STITUTION	OMISSION	INSERTION	TCHR. ASSIST.	SELF-CORRECT.	MEANING DISRUPTION
Popcorn							
There are three major types of							
corn grown in this country.							
First, there is the type of							
corn people eat most of the							
time. It is called sweet corn							
because of its flavor. Second,							
there is field corn, which							
is used mainly for feeding							
livestock. Sometimes people eat field							
corn too. However, its taste							
is not as good as sweet							
corn and its kernels are not							
as full. The third type of corn,							
often called Indian corn, is popcorn.							
Popcorn is grown commercially in the							
United States because the average							
American eats almost two pounds of							
popcorn a year, according //							
to various estimates.							
TOTALS							

Notes:

Examiner's Summary of Miscue Patterns:

PART III: DEVELOPMENTAL/PERFORMANCE SUMMARY

Silent Reading Comprehension

_____ 0–1 questions missed = Easy

_____ 2 questions missed = Adequate

_____ 3+ questions missed = Too hard

Oral Reading Accuracy

_____ 0–1 oral errors = Easy

_____ 2–5 oral errors = Adequate

_____ 6+ oral errors = Too hard

Continue to next assessment level passage? _____ Yes _____ No

Examiner's Notes:

Cooking Without Fire: The Microwave Oven (219 words)

PART I: SILENT READING COMPREHENSION

Background Statement: "This passage is about microwave ovens. Read the selection to find out how microwave ovens were developed. Read it carefully because I'm going to ask you to tell me about what you read."

Teacher Directions: Once the student completes the silent reading, say, "Tell me about the story you just read." Check off any answers to the questions below that the student provides during the retelling. Ask all remaining questions not addressed during the retelling.

Questions/Answers	*Expository Grammar Element/ Level of Comprehension*
_____ 1. What invention led to the development of the microwave oven? *(magnetron tube)*	causation/literal
_____ 2. For what was the magnetron tube first used? *(radar)*	description/literal
_____ 3. What did Dr. Percy Spencer discover about the magnetron tube? *(it could heat food from the inside out)*	description/literal
_____ 4. What was the name given to the first microwave oven? *(Radar Range)*	description/literal
_____ 5. Name two ways that today's microwave ovens differ from the first ones. *(not as bulky, more features, less expensive)*	comparison/inferential
_____ 6. Explain why some people consider microwave cooking the first new method of cooking since the discovery of fire. *(it requires no fire or element of fire to cook food)*	causation/literal
_____ 7. What type of energy is used by the microwave to cook food? *(electromagnetic)*	description/literal
_____ 8. What are two features found on most microwave ovens, according to the passage? *(defrost, reheat, constant temperature cooking)*	description/literal

PART II: ORAL READING AND ANALYSIS OF MISCUES

Directions: Say, "Now I would like to hear you read this story out loud." Have the student read orally until the 100-word sample is completed. Follow along on the Miscue Grid, marking any oral reading errors as appropriate. *Remember to count miscues only up to the point in the story containing the oral reading stop-marker (//).* Then complete the Developmental/Performance Summary to determine whether to continue the assessment. (*Note:* The Miscue Grid should be completed *after* the assessment session has been concluded in order to minimize stress for the student.)

	MIS-PRONUN.	SUB-STITUTION	OMISSION	INSERTION	TCHR. ASSIST.	SELF-CORRECT.	MEANING DISRUPTION
Cooking Without Fire: The							
Microwave Oven							
Microwave cooking is very common							
today. It is, however, a recent invention.							
The microwave oven one uses today							
was developed from the invention							
of the magnetron tube							
in 1940. The invention of							
the magnetron tube, by							
Sir John Randall and Dr. H. A. Boot,							
was a very important part of							
the radar defense of England							
during World War II. Neither man							
considered it as a means of							
preparing food after they invented it.							
It wasn't until the late							
1940s that Dr. Percy Spencer							
discovered the magnetron's ability to							
heat and cook food from							
the inside out. Spencer experimented							
with many different // *foods*,							
all with the same results:							
The inside got hot first.							
TOTALS							

Notes:

Examiner's Summary of Miscue Patterns:

PART III: DEVELOPMENTAL/PERFORMANCE SUMMARY

Silent Reading Comprehension

_____ 0–1 questions missed = Easy

_____ 2 questions missed = Adequate

_____ 3+ questions missed = Too hard

Oral Reading Accuracy

_____ 0–1 oral errors = Easy

_____ 2–5 oral errors = Adequate

_____ 6+ oral errors = Too hard

Continue to next assessment level passage? _____ Yes _____ No

Examiner's Notes:

FORM C: LEVEL 7 ASSESSMENT PROTOCOLS

Diamonds (286 words)

PART I: SILENT READING COMPREHENSION

Background Statement: "The following selection is about diamonds. Read it carefully to find out about how diamonds are made, because I'm going to ask you to tell me all about what you read."

Teacher Directions: Once the student completes the silent reading, say, "Tell me about the story you just read." Check off any answers to the questions below that the student provides during the retelling. Ask all remaining questions not addressed during the retelling.

Questions/Answers	*Expository Grammar Element/ Level of Comprehension*
_____1. Where are the most important diamond fields located? *(India, South America, and Africa)*	description/literal
_____2. What information in the passage supports the idea that diamonds are rare? *(only located in certain areas, and even when present tons of rock must be sorted through)*	problem resolution attempts/ inferential
_____3. Where were the first diamonds found? *(sand and gravel in stream beds)*	description/literal
_____4. On what four things is the quality of a diamond based? *(purity, color, weight, and cut)*	description/literal
_____5. What causes the brilliance of a diamond? *(the way it is cut, or number of facets)*	causation/literal
_____6. What two factors lower the purity of a diamond? *(uncrystallized carbon and foreign substances)*	causation/inferential
_____7. Explain how artificial diamonds are made. *(they result from carbon being placed under high pressure and temperature)*	collection/inferential
_____8. Describe where natural diamonds are found. *(in rock formations that look like volcanoes)*	description/literal

PART II: ORAL READING AND ANALYSIS OF MISCUES

Directions: Say, "Now I would like to hear you read this story out loud." Have the student read orally until the 100-word sample is completed. Follow along on the Miscue Grid, marking any oral reading errors as appropriate. *Remember to count miscues only up to the point in the story containing the oral reading stop-marker (//).* Then complete the Developmental/Performance Summary to determine whether to continue the assessment. (*Note:* The Miscue Grid should be completed *after* the assessment session has been concluded in order to minimize stress for the student.)

	MIS-PRONUN.	SUB-STITUTION	OMISSION	INSERTION	TCHR. ASSIST.	SELF-CORRECT.	MEANING DISRUPTION
Diamonds							
A diamond is one of the							
most beautiful treasures that nature							
ever created, and one							
of the rarest. It takes thousands							
of years for nature to transform							
a chunk of carbon into a rough							
diamond. Only three important							
diamond fields have been found in the							
world—in India, South America,							
and Africa. The first diamonds							
were found in the sand and gravel of							
stream beds. These types of diamonds							
are called alluvial diamonds.							
Later, diamonds were found deep							
in the earth in rock formations called							
pipes. These formations resemble							
extinct volcanoes. The rock in which							
diamonds are found is							
called // *blue ground.*							
TOTALS							

Examiner's Summary of Miscue Patterns:

PART III: DEVELOPMENTAL/PERFORMANCE SUMMARY

Silent Reading Comprehension

_____ 0–1 questions missed = Easy

_____ 2 questions missed = Adequate

_____ 3+ questions missed = Too hard

Oral Reading Accuracy

_____ 0–1 oral errors = Easy

_____ 2–5 oral errors = Adequate

_____ 6+ oral errors = Too hard

Continue to next assessment level passage? _____ Yes _____ No

Examiner's Notes:

FORM C: LEVEL 8 ASSESSMENT PROTOCOLS

The Future Is Here (375 words)

PART I: SILENT READING COMPREHENSION

Background Statement: "This selection is about some inventions that will affect people in the near future. Read it carefully to find out what some of the inventions are and the ways they will affect people because I'm going to ask you to tell me about what you read."

Teacher Directions: Once the student completes the silent reading, say, "Tell me about the story you just read." Check off any answers to the questions below that the student provides during the retelling. Ask all remaining questions not addressed during the retelling.

Questions/Answers	*Expository Grammar Element/ Level of Comprehension*
_____1. What is a levitation vehicle? *(a machine that is part aircraft and part car)*	collection/inferential
_____2. Why are people working on this type of vehicle? *(crowded highways and increase in population)*	causation/literal
_____3. Explain how a dental laser works. *(a laser destroys the cavity without pain)*	description/inferential
_____4. Explain why a full-motion, color video telephone will benefit the deaf. *(the deaf will be able to call people who know sign language and communicate with them)*	causation/inferential
_____5. What do fiber optics do that traditional technology is unable to do? *(allow communication of lots of information over very thin wires)*	comparison/inferential
_____6. What two areas of your current television will be upgraded when high-definition TV becomes common? *(sound and picture)*	description/literal
_____7. What does the sound and picture quality of high-definition TV compare to? *(compact discs and 35-millimeter movies)*	comparison/literal
_____8. What did the passage say about how new advancements will affect people? *(responses will vary but should relate to helping people meet the challenges of the future)*	causation/inferential

PART II: ORAL READING AND ANALYSIS OF MISCUES

Directions: Say, "Now I would like to hear you read this story out loud." Have the student read orally until the 100-word sample is completed. Follow along on the Miscue Grid, marking any oral reading errors as appropriate. *Remember to count miscues only up to the point in the story containing the oral reading stop-marker (//).* Then complete the Developmental/Performance Summary to determine whether to continue the assessment. (*Note:* The Miscue Grid should be completed *after* the assessment session has been concluded in order to minimize stress for the student.)

	MIS-PRONUN.	SUB-STITUTION	OMISSION	INSERTION	TCHR. ASSIST.	SELF-CORRECT.	MEANING DISRUPTION
The Future Is Here							
What will the twenty-first century bring							
in terms of new inventions and							
space-age technologies? No one knows							
for sure. But scientists, inventors, and							
futurists are predicting a variety of new							
inventions. These new advancements							
will affect the way we live and play.							
Some of them are already on the							
drawing board. One example is the							
levitation vehicle. The idea of a vertical							
take-off and landing aircraft that can							
also be driven on the road is the							
invention of Paul Moeller. He named							
his version of this type of craft the							
Moeller 400. People involved in this							
type // *of technology see increases in*							
population and crowded highways as							
reasons that a levitation vehicle							
will be needed.							
TOTALS							

Notes:

Examiner's Summary of Miscue Patterns:

PART III: DEVELOPMENTAL/PERFORMANCE SUMMARY

Silent Reading Comprehension

_____ 0–1 questions missed = Easy

_____ 2 questions missed = Adequate

_____ 3+ questions missed = Too hard

Oral Reading Accuracy

_____ 0–1 oral errors = Easy

_____ 2–5 oral errors = Adequate

_____ 6+ oral errors = Too hard

Continue to next assessment level passage? _____ Yes _____ No

Examiner's Notes:

FORM C: LEVEL 9 ASSESSMENT PROTOCOLS

Visual Illusions (269 words)

PART I: SILENT READING COMPREHENSION

Background Statement: "This selection is about visual illusions. Read it to find out about three specific types of visual illusions. Read it carefully because when you finish I will ask you to tell me about what you have read."

Teacher Directions: Once the student completes the silent reading, say, "Tell me about the story you just read." Check off any answers to the questions below that the student provides during the retelling. Ask all remaining questions not addressed during the retelling.

Questions/Answers	Expository Grammar Element/ Level of Comprehension
_____1. What two reasons were given for visual illusions? *(preconceptions and the brain's difficulty in choosing from two or more patterns)*	description/literal
_____2. What is an example of a lateral inhibition illusion? *(a bull's-eye)*	description/literal
_____3. The Gateway Arch in St. Louis is an example of what distortion? *(length distortion)*	description/literal
_____4. Explain why length distortion occurs. *(because the eyes work better side to side than up and down)*	collection/inferential
_____5. What's an example of the visual illusion called "Hermann's Grid?" *(modern buildings)*	description/literal
_____6. How does Hermann's Grid affect what you see visually? *(it causes the eyes to see gray spots at the corners of squares)*	causation/inferential
_____7. Explain why the old axiom "don't believe everything you see" is valid in everyday life. *(examples of visual illusions are all around us, or other plausible response)*	collection/inferential
_____8. How does the tendency of eyes to move more easily from side to side rather than up and down affect the way we perceive tall objects? *(they seem taller than they actually are)*	causation/literal

PART II: ORAL READING AND ANALYSIS OF MISCUES

Directions: Say, "Now I would like to hear you read this story out loud." Have the student read orally until the 100-word sample is completed. Follow along on the Miscue Grid, marking any oral reading errors as appropriate. *Remember to count miscues only up to the point in the story containing the oral reading stop-marker (//).* Then complete the Developmental/Performance Summary to determine whether to continue the assessment. (*Note:* The Miscue Grid should be completed *after* the assessment session has been concluded in order to minimize stress for the student.)

	MIS-PRONUN.	SUB-STITUTION	OMISSION	INSERTION	TCHR. ASSIST.	SELF-CORRECT.	MEANING DISRUPTION
Visual Illusions							
A visual illusion is an unreal							
or misleading appearance or image,							
according to *Webster's* dictionary. In							
other words, visual illusions are							
sometimes caused by ideas one							
holds about what one expects							
to see. In other instances, the							
illusion is caused by the brain's							
difficulty in choosing from two							
or more visual patterns. If you							
look at a bull's-eye and move							
it slowly in circular motions, you							
should see spokes moving. The							
spokes, if you see them, aren't really							
there. This type of visual illusion is							
called lateral inhibition. Another type							
of visual illusion occurs when a person							
tries to // *estimate the height*							
of a vertical object.							
TOTALS							

Notes:

Examiner's Summary of Miscue Patterns:

PART III: DEVELOPMENTAL/PERFORMANCE SUMMARY

Silent Reading Comprehension

_____ 0–1 questions missed = Easy

_____ 2 questions missed = Adequate

_____ 3+ questions missed = Too hard

Oral Reading Accuracy

_____ 0–1 oral errors = Easy

_____ 2–5 oral errors = Adequate

_____ 6+ oral errors = Too hard

Continue to next assessment level passage? _____ Yes _____ No

Examiner's Notes:

⬛FORM D⬛
Expository Passages
Levels 10–12

Stereo Speakers

Almost everyone has listened to music at one time or another, yet few understand how stereo loudspeakers work. Simply put, all stereo loudspeakers are transducers that change electrical signals from an amplifier into sound waves. Beyond this simplistic explanation, stereo speakers diverge into many different types that even the most enthusiastic music lover can find perplexing. In general, all speakers can be placed into one of two major categories, depending on how the electrical signal is converted to sound.

The most prevalent type of speaker uses *dynamic drivers,* those familiar cones and domes found in both low-cost and expensive models. Basically, this type of speaker has air-exciting diaphragms (cones and domes) that are driven by an electromagnetic component made up of a voice coil and magnet. As an electrical signal is sent from the amplifier, the component moves back and forth. The cone or dome fixed to the voice coil moves with it, resulting in sound waves in the air in front and behind.

The other type of speaker, which produces sound differently from dynamic speakers, is often referred to as a *planar-designed speaker.* This type of speaker, which generally costs substantially more than the dynamic driver type, abandons the use of the voice coil and magnet component in lieu of a flat surface or a long ribbon-like strip that is directly driven by the audio signal from the amplifier to create sound waves. Since most people rarely encounter this type of speaker, the remainder of this discussion will focus on the two major types of dynamic driver speaker.

All dynamic speakers need an enclosure to help prevent something called back wave cancellation. Since all dynamic drivers radiate sound behind as well as in front, if there is no way to control the back wave it will literally cancel out the front wave, resulting in little or no sound. Thus, the enclosure of a stereo speaker serves to deal with this sonic problem.

The most common type of speaker is the acoustic suspension, or sealed box, speaker, which was developed in the 1950s. In this type of speaker, the woofer (dome) is mounted in an airtight enclosure so that its forward surface radiates freely into the room, while its back wave is lost in the internal volume of the sealed box. Since the back wave cannot radiate out into the room, there is no risk of front wave cancellation and it is possible to get powerful bass from a rather diminutive box. The one limitation of this design is that half its acoustical potential (back wave) is lost. Therefore, an acoustic suspension speaker requires more amplifier power than an equivalent unsealed box to achieve a given level of sound.

The other major type of dynamic speaker is called the bass reflex design. This design uses an enclosure that has a carefully designed opening, or vent, which allows the woofer's back wave to escape into the listening area. This type of design tries to capitalize on the back wave by manipulating it so that it reaches the listening area in phase with the front wave. Thus the overall sound is reinforced rather than degraded. This approach produces a more efficient speaker so that, all other things being equal, vented speakers can produce more volume per amplifier watt than acoustic suspension speakers.

Regardless of design, today's speakers far outdistance those of ten years ago in terms of quality of sound per dollar invested. Since no two speakers sound alike regardless of design specifications, the ultimate concern when purchasing a speaker should probably not be design but how it sounds to the individual buyer.

Changing the Way We Look

Cosmetic surgery, once available only to the rich and famous, is a multimillion-dollar-a-year business in the United States. The rapid growth of this type of surgery has occurred even though patients must bear much of the cost, because most cosmetic surgery is not covered by insurance. The cost is considerable, ranging from $1,000 to over $10,000, depending on the procedure, the doctor who does the surgery, and the geographical location in which the procedure is done. Some types of surgery are done on an outpatient basis, while others require several days in the hospital that add to the cost of the procedure.

Most cosmetic surgery is done to modify an individual's facial features. For removal of fine wrinkles around the mouth, brow, and eyes, dermabrasion is often chosen. Dermabrasion requires the physician to use skin planing tools to literally sand off the wrinkled areas after first injecting them with local anesthetic. Smoother skin results, but the patient has to wait about two weeks for the now pinkened skin to return to its normal color.

Another popular facial technique is skin peeling, or chemosurgery. In this procedure, a form of carbolic acid is applied to the face, the top layer of skin is burned off, and a scab results. About ten days later the scab comes off and there is a new, unblemished layer of skin that may take some weeks to return to its normal color. A proscription against direct exposure to the sun for about six months always accompanies this procedure. Fair-skinned individuals are the best candidates because other skin colors may develop irregular pigmentation as a result of this type of surgery.

Eyelid surgery, or blepharoplasty, is done when an individual has excessive skin on the upper lid or bags below the eye. To rid the individual of the "perpetually tired" look, incisions are made in the fold of the lid or just below the lower lash line. Excessive tissue is removed and the incision is stitched. This procedure is usually done on an outpatient basis, and the skin takes only two weeks to return to normal. Although complications are rare, there is always danger of hematomas (puffy areas filled with blood). Also, some people have excessive tearing and some have double vision because of muscle disturbances. Most of these problems either dissipate after several hours or are easily taken care of medically.

Probably the cosmetic surgery most people have heard of is the facelift. Over the past decade, new techniques have been developed so that facelifts can be performed on an outpatient basis. The procedure itself, using local anesthesia along with preoperative sedatives, involves incisions under the hairline and around the ears. Fatty tissue is removed and the loose facial and neck skin is tightened. Sometimes eyelid surgery and chin augmentation accompany the facelift procedure. The recovery time varies from individual to individual but usually lasts several weeks.

Although not everyone is a good candidate for cosmetic surgery, several considerations are worth noting by individuals interested in changing the way they look. First, the choice of an experienced, highly recommended surgeon is a must. Besides plastic or reconstructive surgeons, specialists in dermatology or otolaryngology (ear, nose, and throat) who are board certified can perform cosmetic surgical procedures related to their field of specialization. A second consideration is your expectations: cosmetic surgery can't perform miracles. Although a facial change may be desired, the change you get may or may not meet your initial expectations, so discuss carefully with the doctor what will and won't occur as a result of the surgery. The last consideration is to weigh the expense against the hoped-for results. An old folk saying suggests "don't fix it if it ain't broke." It would seem that many people could save money and pain if they considered carefully whether a change in their looks is really warranted.

Fiber Optic Communications

One of the most important technological advances in recent years has been the advent of fiber optic communications. Whether it is used in an online computer system or an interactive television network, fiber optics is already a part of most Americans' lives. Because it will continue to replace much of what we use to communicate, it is important for people to understand as much as possible about fiber optic communications.

Fiber optic communications is simple: an electrical signal is converted to light, which is transmitted through an optical fiber, which is made of glass, to a distant receiver where it is converted back into the original electrical signal. The advantages of fiber optic communications over other transmission methods are substantial. A signal can be sent over longer distances without being boosted and without interference problems from nearby electrical fields. Additionally, its capacity is far greater than that of copper or coaxial cable systems, and the glass fiber itself is much lighter and smaller than copper systems. Notwithstanding these advantages, fiber optic communications are not problem free.

The most significant limitation in an optical communications system is the attenuation of the optical signal as it goes through the fiber. As information in the light is sent down the fiber, the light is attenuated (often called insertion lost) due to *Rayleigh scattering*. Rayleigh scattering refers to an effect created when a pulse of light is sent down a fiber and part of the pulse is blocked by dopants— microscopic particles in the glass—and scattered in all directions. Some of the light, about 0.0001 percent, is scattered back in the opposite direction of the pulse; this is called the backscatter. Since dopants in optical fiber are uniformly distributed throughout the fiber due to the manufacturing process, this effect occurs along its entire length.

The Rayleigh scattering effect is similar to shining a flashlight in a fog at night. You can see fog because the particles of moisture reflect small amounts of light back at you: the light beam is diffused, or scattered, by the particles of moisture. A thick fog will scatter more of the light because there are more particles to obstruct it. The dopant particles in fiber act like the moisture particles of the fog, returning small amounts of light toward the source as the light hits them. Rayleigh scattering is the major loss factor in fiber optic communications.

Another cause of light loss in optical fiber is *Fresnel reflection*. Fresnel reflection is analogous to shining a flashlight at a window: most of the light passes through the window, but some of it reflects back. The angle at which the light beam hits the window determines whether or not the reflection will bounce back into the flashlight or into your eyes. Whenever light traveling through a material such as optical fiber encounters a material of different density, such as air, some of the light is reflected back toward the light source while the rest continues through the material. In optical fibers these sudden changes occur at the ends of fibers, at fiber breaks, and sometimes at splice joints. Obviously, fiber breaks are of great concern to fiber optic communications companies.

Since fiber optic systems are becoming more expansive and connected over longer distances, it is important to know how much light is lost in a regen, or length, of fiber. It is also important to be able to identify specific points on the fiber that have breaks or signal degradation. Although there are several methods to assess light loss, the most efficient means to pinpoint problems in a regen of fiber is the use of an *optical time domain reflectometer (OTDR).* An OTDR is an electronic optical instrument that can be used to locate defects and faults and to determine the amount of signal loss at any point in an optical fiber by measuring backscatter levels and Fresnel reflection. The OTDR, unlike other methods, only needs access to one end of a fiber to make thousands of measurements along a fiber. The measurement data points can be between 0.5 and 16 meters apart. The selected data points are displayed on the OTDR screen as a line sloping down from left to right, with distance along the horizontal scale and signal level on the vertical scale. Using any two data points, the OTDR can reveal the distance and relative signal levels between them. Thus the OTDR can help companies that own fiber networks to repair breaks and prevent degradation of their signals: in short, to keep communications clear and repairs efficient.

FORM D
Assessment Protocols

FORM D: LEVEL 10 ASSESSMENT PROTOCOLS

Stereo Speakers (605 words)

PART I: SILENT READING COMPREHENSION

Background Statement: "This selection is about stereo speakers. Read it to find out about the different types of speakers that people use to listen to music. Read it carefully because I am going to ask you to tell me what you know about stereo speakers based on the information in the passage."

Teacher Directions: Once the student completes the silent reading, say, "Tell me what you just read about stereo speakers." Check off any answers to the questions below that are provided during the student's retelling of the passage. Ask all remaining questions not addressed during the retelling.

Questions/Answers	Expository Grammar Element/ Level of Comprehension
_____1. What causes sound to come out of a speaker? *(an electrical signal that is changed into sound waves)*	causation/literal
_____2. How are dynamic driver speakers and planar speakers different? *(planar speakers do not use a voice coil/magnet component)*	comparison/inferential
_____3. Why is back wave a problem for makers of stereo speakers? *(if the speaker isn't designed to cope with back wave, the back wave could cancel out the sound)*	causation/literal
_____4. Describe how acoustic suspension speakers eliminate back wave problems. *(they are designed to hold the back wave in the rear of the speaker's sealed enclosure)*	description/inferential
_____5. How is a bass reflex speaker different from a sealed box speaker? *(bass reflex speakers are vented and produce more volume per watt)*	comparison/inferential
_____6. Why would a bass reflex speaker be able to produce more volume per watt? *(because it uses the back wave to help produce the sound rather than canceling the back wave)*	causation/inferential
_____7. Why did the passage suggest that the final choice in buying a speaker should be how it sounds to the buyer rather than design type? *(because all modern speakers are well built but they sound different to different people, so people ought to buy the ones that sound best to them)*	problem resolution/evaluative
_____8. In terms of placement in a room, which type of dynamic driver speaker would be best to place against a wall? *(all things being equal, acoustic suspension speakers would work the best because the bass reflex is vented and needs to be out from the wall)*	problem resolution/evaluative

PART II (OPTIONAL): ORAL READING AND ANALYSIS OF MISCUES

Directions: Say, "Now I would like to hear you read a portion of this passage out loud. Please begin reading with the second paragraph and continue reading until I tell you to stop." Have the student read until the 100-word sample is completed. Follow along on the Miscue Grid, marking any oral reading errors as appropriate. *Remember to count miscues only up to the point of the oral reading stop-marker (///).* Then complete the Developmental/Performance Summary to determine whether to continue the assessment. (Note: The Miscue Grid should be completed *after* the assessment session to save time and reduce stress for the student.)

	MIS-PRONUN.	SUB-STITUTION	OMISSION	INSERTION	TCHR. ASSIST.	SELF-CORRECT.	MEANING DISRUPTION
Stereo Speakers							
The most prevalent type of speaker							
uses dynamic drivers, those familiar							
cones and domes found in both low-							
cost and expensive models. Basically,							
this type of speaker has air-exciting							
diaphragms (cones and domes) that are							
driven by an electromagnetic							
component made up of a voice coil and							
magnet. As an electrical signal is sent							
from the amplifier, the component							
moves back and forth. The cone or							
dome fixed to the voice coil moves							
with it, resulting in sound waves in the							
air in front and behind. The other type							
of speaker, which produces sound							
differently from dynamic speakers, is //							
often referred to as a planar-designed							
speaker.							
TOTALS							

Notes:

Examiner's Summary of Miscue Patterns:

PART III: DEVELOPMENTAL/PERFORMANCE SUMMARY

Silent Reading Comprehension

_____ 0–1 questions missed = Easy

_____ 2 questions missed = Adequate

_____ 3+ questions missed = Too hard

Continue to next assessment level passage? _____ Yes _____ No

Oral Reading Accuracy

_____ 0–1 oral errors = Easy

_____ 2–5 oral errors = Adequate

_____ 6+ oral errors = Too hard

Examiner's Notes:

Changing the Way We Look (649 words)

PART I: SILENT READING COMPREHENSION

Background Statement: "This passage is about cosmetic surgery. Read it carefully and try to find out some facts about different cosmetic surgery techniques, because I am going to ask you to tell me as much as you can remember about the information in the passage."

Teacher Directions: Once the student completes the silent reading, say, "Tell me what you found out about cosmetic surgery." Check off any answers to the questions below that the student provides during the retelling. Ask all remaining questions not addressed during the retelling.

Questions/Answers	*Expository Grammar Element/ Level of Comprehension*
_____1. Describe what is done during dermabrasion. *(the surgeon uses a skin planing tool and scrapes off a layer of skin)*	description/inferential
_____2. What evidence did the passage provide that the number of cosmetic surgery procedures done per year is on the rise? *(it has become a multimillion-dollar business)*	collection/inferential
_____3. How is chemosurgery different from dermabrasion? *(a chemical is used to burn off a layer of skin in chemosurgery while dermabrasion just sands away wrinkles; also chemosurgery results in a scab while dermabrasion does not)*	comparison/inferential
_____4. What are some of the possible complications associated with eyelid surgery? *(hematomas, excessive tearing, and double vision)*	description/literal
_____5. What are three considerations anyone considering plastic surgery should take into account before having it done? *(qualifications of the doctor, cost, and expectations)*	description/literal
_____6. What does the old folk saying suggest about cosmetic surgery? *(Accept responses related to the idea that people should be satisfied with their looks rather than resort to surgery.)*	problem resolution/evaluative
_____7. Besides plastic surgeons, what other kinds of doctors can perform some types of cosmetic surgery? *(dermatologists/skin doctors and otolaryngologists/ ear, nose, and throat doctors)*	collection/literal
_____8. Why does eyelid surgery sometimes accompany a facelift? *(because if a person is having the facial skin tightened, it makes sense to get rid of fatty tissue around the eyes at the same time)*	collection/inferential

PART II (OPTIONAL): ORAL READING AND ANALYSIS OF MISCUES

Directions: Say, "Now I would like to hear you read a portion of this passage out loud. Please begin reading with the third paragraph and continue reading until I tell you to stop." Have the student read until the 100-word sample is completed. Follow along on the Miscue Grid, marking any oral reading errors as appropriate. *Remember to count miscues only up to the point of the oral reading stop-marker (///).* Then complete the Developmental/Performance Summary to determine whether to continue the assessment. (Note: The Miscue Grid should be completed *after* the assessment session to save time and reduce stress for the student.)

	MIS-PRONUN.	SUB-STITUTION	OMISSION	INSERTION	TCHR. ASSIST.	SELF-CORRECT.	MEANING DISRUPTION
Changing the Way We Look							
Another popular facial technique is							
skin peeling, or chemosurgery.							
In this procedure, a form of carbolic							
acid is applied to the face, the top layer							
of skin is burned off, and a scab							
results. About ten days later the scab							
comes off and there is a new,							
unblemished layer of skin that may							
take some weeks to return to its normal							
color. A proscription against direct							
exposure to the sun for about six							
months always accompanies this							
procedure. Fair-skinned individuals							
are the best candidates because other							
skin colors may develop irregular							
pigmentation as a result of this type							
of // surgery.							
TOTALS							

Notes:

Examiner's Summary of Miscue Patterns:

PART III: DEVELOPMENTAL/PERFORMANCE SUMMARY

Silent Reading Comprehension

_____ 0–1 questions missed = Easy

_____ 2 questions missed = Adequate

_____ 3+ questions missed = Too hard

Oral Reading Accuracy

_____ 0–1 oral errors = Easy

_____ 2–5 oral errors = Adequate

_____ 6+ oral errors = Too hard

Continue to next assessment level passage? _____ Yes _____ No

Examiner's Notes:

Fiber Optic Communications (760 words)

PART I: SILENT READING COMPREHENSION

Background Statement: "This selection is about fiber optic communications. Read the passage to discover some of the characteristics and problems associated with fiber optic communications. Read it carefully because I am going to ask you to tell me about the entire passage when you finish reading it."

Teacher Directions: Once the student completes the silent reading, say, "Tell me as much as you can remember about fiber optic communications." Check off all answers to the questions below that the student provides during the retelling. Ask all remaining questions not addressed during the retelling.

Questions/Answers	*Expository Grammar Element/ Level of Comprehension*
_____1. What two advantages does fiber optics have over other forms of communications transmission? *(no interference problems, does not need boosting over long distances, greater capacity, lighter and smaller)*	collection/literal
_____2. What are dopants? *(microscopic particles found in all optic fibers)*	description/literal
_____3. Why is loss of light in optic fiber a major concern of companies that uses it for communication? *(poor signals or even a complete system shutdown)*	problem resolution/evaluative
_____4. What is Rayleigh scattering and why is it always present? *(the light that is reflected back toward its source due to dopants; because of the manufacturing process)*	causation/literal
_____5. Explain the main difference between Rayleigh scattering and Fresnel reflection. *(Rayleigh scattering caused by dopants, Fresnel reflection caused by fiber breaks, splices, or the end of fiber; accept plausible responses even if related to the fog versus light through glass analogy)*	comparison/inferential
_____6. How are a regen and an optical time domain reflectometer related? *(OTDR used to pinpoint light loss in any regen)*	collection/inferential
_____7. What separates the OTDR from other devices designed to pinpoint loss of light in fiber optic cable? *(only need access to one end of a fiber to make measurements)*	comparison/literal
_____8. Why would it be safe to say that OTDRs and other devices will be in greater demand in the future than they are now? *(because of the expansion of fiber optic communications)*	collection/evaluative

PART II (OPTIONAL): ORAL READING AND ANALYSIS OF MISCUES

Directions: Say, "Now I would like to hear you read a portion of this passage out loud. Please begin reading with the third paragraph and continue reading until I tell you to stop." Have the student read until the 100-word sample is completed. Follow along on the Miscue Grid, marking any oral reading errors as appropriate. *Remember to count miscues only up to the point of the oral reading stop-marker (///).* Then complete the Developmental/Performance Summary to determine whether to continue the assessment. (Note: The Miscue Grid should be completed *after* the assessment session to save time and reduce stress for the student.)

	MIS-PRONUN.	SUB-STITUTION	OMISSION	INSERTION	TCHR. ASSIST.	SELF-CORRECT.	MEANING DISRUPTION
Fiber Optic Communications							
The most significant limitation in an							
optical communications system is the							
attenuation of the optical signal as it							
goes through the fiber. As information							
in the light is sent down the fiber, the							
light is attenuated (often called							
insertion lost) due to *Rayleigh*							
scattering. Rayleigh scattering refers							
to an effect created when a pulse of							
light is sent down a fiber and part of							
the pulse is blocked by dopants—							
microscopic particles in the glass—							
and scattered in all directions. Some of							
the light, about 0.0001 percent, is							
scattered back in the opposite direction							
of the pulse; this is called the //							
backscatter.							
TOTALS							

Notes:

Examiner's Summary of Miscue Patterns:

PART III: DEVELOPMENTAL/PERFORMANCE SUMMARY

Silent Reading Comprehension

_____ 0–1 questions missed = Easy

_____ 2   questions missed = Adequate

_____ 3+   questions missed = Too hard

Oral Reading Accuracy

_____ 0–1 oral errors = Easy

_____ 2–5 oral errors = Adequate

_____ 6+   oral errors = Too hard

Examiner's Notes:

APPENDIX
ADDITIONAL MISCUE GRIDS

ADDITIONAL MISCUE GRID FOR READERS IN GRADES 1 THROUGH 12

	MIS-PRONUN.	SUB-STITUTION	OMISSION	INSERTION	TCHR. ASSIST.	SELF-CORRECT.	MEANING DISRUPTION
TOTALS							

Notes:

Examiner's Summary of Miscue Patterns:

PART III: DEVELOPMENTAL/PERFORMANCE SUMMARY

Silent Reading Comprehension

_____ 0–1 questions missed = Easy

_____ 2 questions missed = Adequate

_____ 3+ questions missed = Too hard

Oral Reading Accuracy

_____ 0–1 oral errors = Easy

_____ 2–5 oral errors = Adequate

_____ 6+ oral errors = Too hard

Continue to next assessment level passage? _____ Yes _____ No

Examiner's Notes:

ADDITIONAL MISCUE GRID FOR READERS IN GRADES 1 THROUGH 12

	MIS-PRONUN.	SUB-STITUTION	OMISSION	INSERTION	TCHR. ASSIST.	SELF-CORRECT.	MEANING DISRUPTION
TOTALS							

Examiner's Summary of Miscue Patterns:

PART III: DEVELOPMENTAL/PERFORMANCE SUMMARY

Silent Reading Comprehension

_____ 0–1 questions missed = Easy

_____ 2 questions missed = Adequate

_____ 3+ questions missed = Too hard

Oral Reading Accuracy

_____ 0–1 oral errors = Easy

_____ 2–5 oral errors = Adequate

_____ 6+ oral errors = Too hard

Continue to next assessment level passage? _____ Yes _____ No

Examiner's Notes:

ADDITIONAL MISCUE GRID FOR READERS IN GRADES 1 THROUGH 12

	MIS-PRONUN.	SUB-STITUTION	OMISSION	INSERTION	TCHR. ASSIST.	SELF-CORRECT.	MEANING DISRUPTION
TOTALS							

Examiner's Summary of Miscue Patterns:

PART III: DEVELOPMENTAL/PERFORMANCE SUMMARY

Silent Reading Comprehension

_____ 0–1 questions missed = Easy

_____ 2   questions missed = Adequate

_____ 3+   questions missed = Too hard

Continue to next assessment level passage? _____ Yes _____ No

Oral Reading Accuracy

_____ 0–1 oral errors = Easy

_____ 2–5 oral errors = Adequate

_____ 6+   oral errors = Too hard

Examiner's Notes: